Something Extraordinary
An Inspirational Journal Sparked by Cancer

By

Loni Kaplan

Copyright © 2013 Loni Kaplan

All rights reserved.

ISBN-13:978-14840008515

DEDICATION

To my driving force, the reason I became who I am, my four wonderful boys, Adam, Jaron, Evan and Derek. May the lessons herein inform your lives and help you know how your mother has seen the world.

DONATIONS

My purpose in writing this book is to share my story with and inspire as wide an audience as possible. I would also like to take this opportunity to share my good fortune with others.

I will be donating a minimum of 50% of the profits of the book sales to the following organizations. I believe these organizations do good work and help many people. These are the causes in which I believe:

1. Lung Cancer Alliance — lungcanceralliance.org

2. Faces of Courage Cancer Camps — facesofcourage.wordpress.com

3. Profoundly Gifted Retreat — pgretreat.com

4. LIFE of Tampa Homeschool (a national group) — lifeoftampa.blogspot.com

5. Habitat for Humanity — habitat.org

6. Heifer International — heifer.org

ACKNOWLEDGMENTS

When I completed the manuscript for this book, I reached out to my PG Retreat family to be my copy editors. There was a tremendously generous outpouring of offers to help, some from people I had not yet met. I thank my team of copy editors, without whom this book would not be possible.

December 5, 2010

One week ago, I was having dinner at a Thai restaurant with two dear friends. We were laughing and sharing stories as always.

Tomorrow, I begin chemotherapy and radiation for aggressive lung cancer. While my life has turned upside down over the course of a few days, I am hopeful, optimistic and beyond grateful for the outpouring of love, light and support I have already received from my friends and my community.

While we may never understand why or how this is happening, I do firmly believe that everything is for a reason, and whatever lessons we are all meant to learn will come to us all…

For the past two months, I have been experiencing dizziness. While I was certainly concerned and worried, dizziness has so many etiologies that it could have been anything.

Twenty years ago, I was diagnosed with Benign Paroxysmal Positional Vertigo (BPPV) due to fainting spells. I had a complete work-up at the Balance Institute at the University of South Florida (USF) and was told it was something I would have all my life.

Due to the stresses of the previous few months (I had separated from Todd after 21 years of marriage), I just assumed that the primary cause of the problem was stress.

I have also had sinus and allergy issues for over ten years, so assumed the problems were again related. However, this was different. I had a severe bout of vertigo on October 5 which left the room spinning, the bed spinning, and me spinning. I was able to sleep it off and be functional the next day.

Each day, I was a little off. I had a bit of trouble walking and just didn't feel right. I began antibiotics for what I knew was a sinus infection. I saw my ear, nose and throat doctor (ENT) who cultured my infection and did a series of tests on my inner ear to see if there were any obvious problems. Everything was clear. He recommended treating the sinus infection first, and then, if I was still having trouble, we would further investigate the dizziness.

On November 1, I began prednisone, a steroid, along with the antibiotics. The change in how I felt was remarkably dramatic. Not only was I stable physically for the first time in weeks, but my whole mood, demeanor and stance changed as well. I was optimistic, light, laughing, giddy, joyous.

I felt glorious for two weeks and hoped I had turned a corner and was simply dealing better with the stresses in my life. I went to the I Can Do It! conference in Tampa and immersed myself in the positive energy I found there. I had weaned off the steroids at that point, and on Sunday, when I was ready to go to the conference, I could barely move. I went back to bed and slept until 11. I drove myself to the conference anyway, wanting to pick up some items I had purchased from the vendors. I went to one lecture, but could not even sit up. My whole body was crunched in an effort to be stable. I lay on the floor in the back listening and drove myself home afterward. I went straight to bed.

I called the next morning for more prednisone. It was the only difference I could determine in what I had done. Upon taking the first pill, I felt the lightness in my head solidify down to the ground. I felt grounded again and solid. Again, my mood lightened.

A few days later, I saw some people I had last seen when I was dizzy. The difference in me was striking to them as well. I was told my eyes were clear, my voice was light and laughing, I was smiling. My lawyer told me I should be the poster child for "Divorce Doesn't Have to Ruin Your Life," as she had never had a client as optimistic and hopeful about her life, or exuding as much joy as I did. She commented on my glowing skin and the light in my eyes.

I was nearing the end of the second course of prednisone, and I was afraid. I worried the dizziness would return and I knew I could not remain on steroids forever. Friends on Facebook helped do my medical sleuthing, and suggested various possibilities, including Lyme disease and ear surgeries.

I finished my last pill Thanksgiving morning, and spent a delightful, relaxing day at a dear friend's house with the kids. I was so comfortable that I even took an after-dinner nap on her couch.

On Friday morning, I woke up dizzy. I dropped my car off for service, and got a ride to the house to be with the kids, as I did every day. As the day went on, I got worse. I went to lie down in bed, and was throwing up by the afternoon. I called the ENT, who asked me to come in Monday morning, at which time he would order an MRI.

Since Todd is a radiologist, I was able to get an MRI at any time. I thought it would help to have the information up front, so I went at 8:30 on Monday morning, when they kindly squeezed me in between patients. After my

MRI, I drove to the ENT's office. I stopped for breakfast, as I had not eaten, at which time Todd called and told me the scan was very abnormal. He had not yet seen it, but told me to go to the ENT's office right away. Todd called me back after he had seen the MRI and told me I was at immediate risk of a seizure as my brain was quite swollen, and that the ENT would send me straight to the hospital. He had already spoken to the neurosurgeon. It looked like either a brain infection or metastases. I cried as I walked into the ENT's office and was rushed through.

I drove across the street to the ER and was admitted right away. The technician took a chest x-ray, as is done routinely upon admittance. Todd joined me. He had called my parents as soon as he saw the MRI and they were already on their way.

The doctor immediately put me on anti-seizure medication, along with further steroids. As I was waiting to get the CT scan of my chest, abdomen and pelvis to search for the primary tumor, my ENT came into the room to see me. "I'm so sorry," he said. He had just seen my chest x-ray, which showed a large mass in my right lung. I cried as I was wheeled down the hall. Todd went with my ENT to see the x-ray as I went for my CT. Thankfully, the doctor saw no additional spots on any of the CT scans. I went to the surgical ICU unit and waited.

I was scheduled for a bronchoscopy the next morning as well as a thoracotomy in the afternoon in case they could not get enough tissue from the bronchoscopy to biopsy the mass in my lung. Thankfully, they were able to get enough and I did not have to have my chest cut open! Now it was a matter of waiting. I had texted a number of friends Monday afternoon when I was admitted and again after the biopsy. Everyone sent love and light, prayers and support. The energy was palpable, especially from my wonderful Facebook support group, Good Karma Mama, which has done miraculous manifesting (helping bring positive intentions to fruition) for its participants. I knew I would stay positive and not yet worry about the diagnosis.

Wednesday afternoon, at 4 p.m., Todd and my mother walked into the room, along with the oncologist who had been following my case. The oncologist confirmed that it was lung cancer. I began to cry and asked a few questions. He left us and came back about ten minutes later when I could think clearly enough to ask a few more questions.

Todd stayed with me until about 9 p.m. that night. He has been amazing throughout this experience. He told me that all decisions are mine, and that I am welcome to move back into the house, in the guest suite. Since I could no longer drive because of the risk of seizures, and would have to have constant care, my parents could stay at the house and take care of the children.

I had a port put in my chest Thursday morning so that chemotherapy could begin right away. I was released from the hospital Thursday afternoon and went back to the house.

We had planned to tell the kids together, but Todd was out getting my medicine and the kids came in to me, asking questions. They knew that I had had a biopsy, but didn't know yet whether it was an infection or cancer. I told them the truth, as I always have and always will.

I explained that it was lung cancer and that we would begin treatment right away. Jaron told me that he had online friends who had been praying for me.

Derek asked, "So if you're going to get treatment, you're not going to die, right?" I talked more about the treatment, but did not address the second half of the question. Neither he nor Evan seemed to realize it, but Jaron did immediately.

Friday morning, I went for a PET scan to see if the cancer had traveled further. Beautiful news...it was "only" in my lung and brain. This was amazing and hopeful news! I went to the oncologist and was fitted for my radiation mask and given chemo education. Everyone was wonderful as they explained the process.

Saturday, Todd's wonderful friends, along with Todd and Jaron, moved me out of the apartment. They were supportive and kind and never made me feel awkward about the situation. They matter-of-factly packed up my stuff and brought it to the house.

As we drove back, Todd said how sorry he was that the apartment didn't work out for me beyond the two months. I explained how freeing it had been living there, and he understood. I had been on my own for the first time in over twenty years, with no responsibility to anyone but myself. I went to bed when I wanted and didn't have to worry about getting anyone ready but myself. It had been a light, happy time. I was sad and emotional about packing everything up (I had chosen minimal furnishings, as I wanted little: only a couch, a bed and a computer).

I have set up the guest suite at our house as my own apartment, with my own computer and desk. The bed and couch went up to the Wii room and the kids know they are absolutely welcome to come and be with me, but they need to ask, as I need to rest a lot.

Once I began sending emails to people who did not know, I again felt enveloped in the love and support of all. People I had not been in touch with for years reached out to send wishes, prayers, hugs. Wonderful friends are researching alternative, adjunct therapies.

While I do plan on sticking to traditional therapies, I am completely open to adding anything that can't hurt. The amount of information and misinformation, of course, is beyond overwhelming, so friends sorting through it all is a tremendous help, which I will gratefully accept.

A wonderful friend set up a *Lotsa Helping Hands* website,

which allows people to sign up for shifts to drive me to doctors' appointments as well as bring dinners.

I gratefully look forward to everyone's love, light and support as I travel this journey. I know I am not alone and that whatever lessons we are all meant to learn throughout will become clear, or not. We may just be meant to travel the path…

December 7

I am humbled, honored and beyond blown away by the tremendous support, love, light and outpouring by each and every one of you.

140 visits to my CaringBridge page each day…you are all remarkable.

My wonderful rabbi came and sat with me yesterday as I was being infused with the chemotherapy through my port, and I shared with him what I will share with you all.

You never know how you touch people's lives. Yes, there are some with whom you are fortunate enough to have an instant connection, and those are the deep and meaningful relationships of our lives, even if they may be with those who are far away or not often seen. While those people hold such a deep and special place in our hearts, there are others who are also important.

There are people whom you may have met only once, yet who make an impression and touch you in some way. Or people who seem to merely be casual acquaintances, yet in reality, are so much more.

I feel incredibly fortunate to be surrounded by all these people. People have shared with me the impact I have had on their lives, and I am awed by the generosity and spirit with which their recollections are shared.

When my mother turned 60, my brother, sister and I gave her a gift which we hoped would be beyond measure. We contacted people from all times of her life and asked them to share stories and recollections of their relationship. She loved them all. I strongly encourage each of you, as your loved ones have a milestone coming up, to do the same for them. Don't wait until you have a reason like mine.

I am being given such a gift right now, and I want you each to know the tremendous strength your stories, your words, your kindnesses are giving me.

I am awed, grateful and so incredibly thankful.

December 9

Back in June, I read a book called *How to be a People Magnet*. It was fun and light, but had a wonderful section about building your community. The author had experienced a health crisis and discovered how much she relied on her friends to help her through. She also discovered that the time to build your community is when you don't actively need it. She referred to her community resources—auto mechanics, plumbers, handymen, general go-to people—for everything.

When I had first moved to the apartment, I consciously worked to create the community that helped me then. My friend's husband came and helped me set up my computer. Another friend helped me bring in some furniture. I reached out to people I had not connected with in a while to have breakfast on a Sunday morning, and through Facebook, reconnected with friends I worked with twenty years ago.

These people and so many more have been incredibly supportive and I continue to be amazed and awed by you all. My wonderful PG Retreat family...I feel your love from every corner of the country, and am so grateful for the words, warmth and lovely care packages you are sending my way.

I am grateful to have the time to visit with my friends as they generously take the time to drive me to my doctors' appointments. An appointment time was extended over lunch on Tuesday as a friend and I visited and caught up with each other's lives: a gentle reminder to all of us to take the time and focus on the people in our lives. As anyone who has ever been out with me knows, I like to close down the restaurant whenever we go out, so am grateful for hours to talk and visit with my friends!

Last night, I had the privilege of having dinner with a dear old friend with whom I worked twenty years ago. We shared laughter and reminiscences along with life philosophy. While we did talk about the cancer, it was just one topic among many. My friend had always been a gentle soul, but time has added to his wisdom and I felt honored to be surrounded by his light.

This morning, I didn't have to be out the door by 9 a.m. for chemo, so I was able to actually make my own breakfast and putter around a little bit. The kids went to play at a friend's house and we were all ever-so-grateful for that distraction.

Since the anticipation is that I will become more fatigued as treatment goes on, I am planning to take advantage of the energy I still have left and go with the kids to Pokémon tournaments this weekend on the East Coast. We had planned the trip before we knew anything was wrong, and we want to maintain as much normalcy as possible. And this way, I'll get to visit with my wonderful Pokémon friends from around the state!

Loni Kaplan

Thank you to everyone for your continuing light and love...I feel it surrounding me every moment and am ever so grateful.

December 13

I will post an update about my wonderful weekend soon, but just want everyone to know that right now, I feel like Forrest Gump. Each morning, I feel that life is indeed "a box of chocolates," and I am very grateful to open the box anew each day and be delighted by the surprises I find.

Generous, thoughtful and amazing care packages have been arriving by mail, UPS and FedEx each day, along with CaringBridge guestbook messages, emails and Facebook messages in which people just astound me with the depth and kindness of their words. Each day I discover which wonderful friend has kindly offered to drive me to my doctors' appointment and spend the time chatting with me, which I so love. I am enjoying the culinary skills of friends who have broadened my family's palate while respectfully ensuring that we are happily nourished.

December 14

Musings from a Pokémon Weekend

The "Sponge Bob" song, "Best Day Ever," keeps playing in my head. We just got back from a weekend of Pokémon in Port St. Lucie and Melbourne, Florida, and it was one of a few "best weekends ever."

I have been blessed with four magical weekends in the past two years. The first was Adam's Bar Mitzvah. The second, a Pokémon tournament in Port St. Lucie when cousin Jake was with us. The third, Virginia Regionals when Derek won. And the fourth was this weekend. Three of four were Pokémon weekends, when I just felt this incredible sense of peace and alignment; the universe was raining grace. I felt utter joy, peace and sheer contentment coursing through me.

Pokémon, along with being a TV cartoon, is a popular card game with tournaments throughout the country and the world. My kids started playing about two years ago. At their urging, I began playing six months later.

I love these tournaments in Port St. Lucie! Two of the biggest-hearted people I know are the tournament organizers, and there is just something magical about these particular venues. Background history of these venues: this was our fourth time there.

Something Extraordinary

The first time we went to Port St. Lucie, Derek met a man who would become his mentor of sorts in the game. He had just turned seven, and he watched with interest as this man played a match for fun with his son. Derek asked if he could play him next. The man kindly agreed, and they struck up a friendship. He was engaging with Derek; he talked with him about the card decks he had built and asked lots of questions. As the years have gone by, we found that he built decks the way Derek did. He liked many of the same cards and disliked playing others. He has been an excellent sounding board for all my kids, and he is a world-class player.

The second time we went, my nephew came to join us from New York. He was our good luck charm. Derek won all his matches that day, losing only in top cut. More miraculously, I won every game I played except to a world-class player to whom I lost three times. That weekend, I played top cut both days, placing second and third place. As in many games, when you are good, people notice you and develop a certain level of respect for your play. That weekend, I met many people because I did well and people wanted to know about my deck and get ideas from me. When I saw them at subsequent tournaments throughout the year, they remembered me from that weekend. I had played a rogue deck then, which I always like doing. I do not play the standard meta-game decks as I find them boring and unimaginative.

Fast-forward to this past weekend.

Bottom line numbers: Derek won both Cities tournaments, Evan placed third. In Jaron's age division, he top cut (placed in a top position to be eligible to play to win the tournament) Saturday to place second and came in fifth to miss top cut by a fraction of an opponent's opponent's win percentage (miniscule accounting amount). I came in sixth both days, including playing top cut on Sunday. Todd finished last on Saturday, but top cut to seventh on Sunday.

Pokémon, for those who do not play the game, seems like a kids' game. It is actually an incredibly complicated, strategic and cerebral competition. The thrill of figuring out exactly which combination of cards to play when, figuring out how to play your deck when what you need is prized, figuring out how many more turns you have to play your active Pokémon while retreating strategically...it is a real thought exercise.

Except for a few games at the Pokémon League we run each week, which meets at Burger King, and a few games at home with the kids, I had not played since August at Worlds in Hawaii. I played the same deck I had played in June with a few minor edits. But when I played on Saturday, it all came back. I won my first round to a deck that should have been an auto-loss. I played until time and figured out ways around the trainer-lock in which I was put. The second round, I played a young man I had met last year in Port St. Lucie during the first Best Weekend Ever there.

My second round play was a mirror-match but with several differences. My techs were different than his, and we also played to time, prize for prize. We were down to two prizes to one, and I knew he would win. But watching his strategy to claim that last prize card was invigorating and enlightening.

The third round was just before lunch. I knew I was playing a little slower and the cards weren't making as much sense to me. I misplayed a few cards (nothing major, just not the best thought-out choice, which happens plenty to people with clear minds, too) and called an attack or two without the right energy. My opponent just couldn't draw any energy, so I was able to keep attacking without getting knocked out. I again played to time and was at six prizes to two. I didn't even pay attention to who the active player was when time was called, as I knew that I would win regardless.

After the match, my opponent asked the judge if there was a time limit on turns, as I took a really long time to play. He said yes, generally two minutes, but explained that there were some extenuating circumstances in my case. He explained that I had just been diagnosed with cancer and had begun my chemo and radiation treatments just this week. I had been happy to be able to come and play at all, and was doing my best.

We broke for lunch and I went to rest on a comfortable chair. I visited with a dear friend whom I had not seen in almost a year and shared my story with him. As we were speaking, I heard in the play room that they were about to announce the Junior standings. I wanted to get a picture of Derek winning his first Cities medal, so I went to run into the room. I forgot that my balance doesn't work very well right now, and my leg must have fallen asleep. I got up out of the chair and stumbled as I went to run, falling down on the floor. I fell on my hip and just lay there stunned for a few moments. I was fine, everyone came running to help me up, and I got my camera shots as Derek and Evan were presented with their prizes.

After I ate lunch, I felt much better. I thought I would have to drop at lunch, but decided to play the afternoon, as Jaron was in top cut anyway, and I was feeling better after eating and resting. I lost my next match to a match-up that is an auto-loss and then won my final round. I placed sixth out of 25 players.

After dinner, we went back to the hotel and I stopped in the lobby to post news of the day on Facebook and catch up on emails. When I had not returned to the room an hour later, Jaron came down to the lobby to make sure I was okay. He kept close tabs on me all weekend, making sure I had plenty to drink and checking if I needed anything. Evan does the same thing at home; they are taking such great care of me!

On Sunday, we showed up at the venue at 9:30 a.m., as the website had listed the incorrect start times. We called and found out it we didn't need to be there until 11:30, so we went to Barnes & Noble for a couple of hours. Todd played cards with the kids; I sat and read quietly. I was feeling some strange tingling sensations in my body, and just a little off. Though I had eaten breakfast before we left the hotel, I thought I would probably do better if I ate every few hours, so I had lunch before the tournament started.

I won the first two matches in one and two turns (called a donk in Pokémon lingo) and Derek and Evan both won their first two matches as well, so would play each other in Round 3 as they often do. Sometimes, Evan has offered Derek the win, but more often, they play it out. They did play it out, and Derek donked Evan to go on to win the medal.

We broke for lunch and ate pizza. I met a history teacher and we shared stories of unique ways to engage the kids with role plays and different takes on modern problems. I rarely get to speak of my passion for teaching history during a Pokémon competition, so was thrilled to meet someone who shared my enthusiasm.

In Round 3, I again played the young man whom I had met last year. We spoke of his college interests: nursing, animation and physics. Pokémon is not for the intellectual lightweight. Through Pokémon, I have met a young man who went on to attend Yale, as well as several engineers and lawyers. There are also many who play who have the intellectual capacity for the incredible intricacies of the game, and are challenged by it because they don't necessarily get the intellectual stimulation from their jobs..

These are intelligent, interesting people whom I thoroughly enjoy.

This is one of the main reasons my kids love the game. While Derek and Evan do get frustrated by some of the kids who don't get it, they have met a lot of very smart kids who play and they can relate well to them. Derek knows kids around the country whom he considers his friends, although he may have only met them once or twice (at the Georgia Marathon, both Florida and New York States, Virginia Regionals—which he won, Nationals in Indianapolis and Worlds tournaments in both San Diego and Hawaii).

The local paper ran a wonderful story last year about Pokémon tournaments, which included Derek and a dear friend of my boys. The journalist explained how her homeschooled son thrived in the environment, as have mine. There are so many life lessons to be learned from the game in addition to the play: not cheating, being clear about your play, speaking kindly to your opponent, always calling a judge if there is any question, respectfully stating your case and standing up for what you know is right, even when you are only eight years old and an adult is telling you something you know is incorrect. We have gone over many scenarios after matches, and each time they play, the kids learn something new, just as often in interpersonal skills as in the game itself. The game can help build character, and you can spot a kid with character as soon as you sit down.

Derek is fond of saying he plays to win, but he mostly plays for fun. He will always let his opponent take back a mistake as long as he or she is nice to him and allows him to do the same.

Back to this weekend again.

I played Round 3 prize for prize. My opponent had a few key cards prized, so he had to rethink his strategy. I loved watching him figure out how he would do it. Since we had played the day before, we knew each other's decks completely. We played almost until time: another excellent match which he won at 2-1 prizes.

I won my fourth round fairly easily, but with a few different strategies. I ate a protein bar (eating every two hours helped a lot!). I was 3-1 going in to the last round. We took prize for prize, and I won in sudden death.

I was 4-1 and in top cut! Todd got dinner for me (he was in top cut for the first time, too). I lost the first game, won the second, and lost the third in an incredibly exciting match, again played all the way to time. I was so clear exactly how to play. My mind was incredibly focused and I saw strategies I do not think I normally would have.

As I savored an excellent match well played (the judge said he really enjoyed watching, as it was truly a thinking game for both of us!), I announced with gratitude that I didn't know when I would get to play again due to my treatments, but that I had had an incredible weekend of excellent competition, excellent friends, terrific support and the intellectual stimulation that I think can only help knock out the cancer in my brain.

I have been an avid supporter of Pokémon for the last two years, running a league with my kids, traveling the country to tournaments, enjoying wonderful friendships with such interesting people. I have learned much and hope to have many more opportunities to give back.

December 20

I am inspired by the feedback I have received from my Pokémon musings post. I told Pokémon International they should put me on payroll! Really, I am glad to be able to share our love for the game and help everyone understand what it is all about, and some of what we are all about as well.

I will share more big-picture journaling with you all shortly, but do want to post a more factual update in the meantime.

We went away again this past weekend: we attended two more Pokémon tournaments in Orlando. I almost didn't want to go, as I feared it would be a disappointment after the joy of last weekend, but in the past, we always went to all the tournaments regardless, and I was feeling well enough to travel, so off we went.

I am certainly glad we went; we saw a different group of friends and shared different experiences. Jaron top cut again to take second place Saturday. Derek took fourth Saturday and Evan sixth both days. Much to Derek's chagrin but Evan's joy, Evan beat Derek both days in the first round. They always decide between themselves whether they will play it out or Evan will give Derek the win. It teaches them both many lessons when they do play it out; I'm glad they work it out between them.

I was 2-3 Saturday and 3-2 Sunday, so it was a balanced weekend. I had a few great matches and again, enjoyed the mental challenge of figuring it all out.

Last week, we went for a consultation at Moffitt Cancer Center in Tampa. The facility where I am being treated is affiliated with Moffitt, but they recommend getting a second opinion nonetheless. We met with a thoracic oncologist, who confirmed the treatment plan I am currently undergoing. We also spoke of a clinical trial that I would be eligible to participate in once my current treatment plan is complete.

I do not want to get into any healthcare debates or complaints about the way medicine must be practiced. Suffice it to say that the frustration of knowing you can participate in a clinical trial and just get a placebo is looming. However, as the doctor pointed out, if you don't participate, you have zero percent chance of getting any treatment, whereas if you do participate, you get a fifty percent (or in this case, a 66 percent) chance of getting additional treatment. Aah, the FDA...

There have been tremendous advances in cancer research, with vaccines and antibodies. But small cell lung cancer, which I have, does not yet have any additional medical treatment beyond the standard and what is in trials. So we go from there...

Except for some severe knee pain and sleeplessness I have been experiencing, I am continuing to feel well. My appetite hasn't been better in years (thank you, steroids!). We went to Golden Corral for dinner on Saturday and I ate almost three plates of food! I haven't eaten this much since I was pregnant with Derek and Evan! But I know my appetite will be short-lived, so am getting in all the good calories I can.

I told my doctor that I was hungry all the time, and had gotten trail mix to sustain me for a long car ride. He laughed and said he would have chosen donuts! I continue to try to choose well and healthy.

My hair is starting to fall out as of this morning's shower. I have very thick hair, so may have another day or two of pulling out handfuls before it's noticeable. But I do plan to take some "last old hair" photos with the kids today.

Great thanks to all who are coming to visit me throughout the month of January...friends far and wide reaching out so selflessly. I will continue to book my calendar as long as I have the energy to visit. Throughout my younger years, I always tested as an extrovert on the Myers-Briggs personality type test. As I got older, I wondered if perhaps I was really a closet introvert, as I found myself not wanting to be with people quite as much. I see now that there is no doubt. I clearly draw my energy from being with others. I am always invigorated after a visit with dear friends, and am grateful to everyone for sharing your positive energies with me.

December 23

The Road Less Traveled

Two roads diverged in a yellow wood.
And I —I took the one less traveled by,
and that has made all the difference.

—Robert Frost

I first memorized this poem in seventh grade, and loved it immediately. I can't say I chose at that time to live my life this way, but it has informed my choices and decisions, and looking back, I find that I have indeed made the less conventional choices, at least much of the time. And that has, indeed, made all the difference. (For those to whom the homeschooling part does not apply, feel free to skip down...there is a part very applicable to you, too! I will warn you that some of my conclusions may feel uncomfortable to some of you, particularly those who are more societally/conventionally bound; I offer them unabashedly and candidly, without rancor.)

Homeschooling is the most obvious "outside-the-box" choice I have made. While I had never even heard of homeschooling before Adam was four years old, I quickly embraced the lifestyle and enjoyed being outside the norm. When a family first starts homeschooling, it often leans more towards school-at-home, as that approximates a comfort level with which parents are most familiar from their own childhood. Over time, as parents see what works and what doesn't, they develop more confidence in their own abilities, and tend toward a less school-y approach.

Adam ensured that we got there a lot quicker. He is the ideal child to homeschool. He is self-motivated, academically inclined, and interested in everything. From day one, he let me know what worked for him and what didn't. And I always honored his path. The first few years were certainly the hardest, as I had to fight societal conventions about age. I consistently placed him in classes or opportunities that were listed for those above his age, and he always thrived. I never lied about his age, nor did I make apologies. I simply stated that the particular opportunity was the right one for him, and most of the time, was able to convince the instructors to give him a chance. No one was ever disappointed. I developed a sense of confidence in bucking the norm, for I saw that it turned out well. A calm sense of acceptance that things are the way they are applies across the board.

I am intensely proud of the person Adam has become. He has followed his own path from the start, and has found his community. The bridge (competitive card game) world suits him perfectly; he engages with brilliant minds daily and is thoroughly challenged at every step of the way. He thrives in that environment, and we encourage his growth and independence as he is exactly who he was meant to be.

When I could not find classes or resources that were appropriate, I simply created my own. This seems like an obvious solution to me, yet I know it would not work for everyone. Why sit around and complain about what does not exist when you can make it exist? This strategy began with Jaron. He was very interested in geography. He was in a Montessori school at the time, and while they did let him participate in the geography bee when he was five years old, I saw that he needed a more in-depth study than was available to him. I created my own class, which I taught at the library across the street from his school. Each week, I pulled him out for the hour I taught, and he got a little taste of homeschooling.

It took him two more years to choose to homeschool full-time, but throughout that period, I continued to teach a geography class to prep for geography, spelling and vocabulary bees for the homeschool community. I discovered I loved to teach in a very out-of-the-box way. Each class I taught held a different theme: one year, we did a road rally in which I split the class in two sections and we raced around the world. Another year, the theme was immigration to America, beginning tens of thousands of years ago, in which the students each researched their own family tree, and which later became the basis for Adam's Bar Mitzvah project.

I took that same immigration class to a homeschool co-op, and began teaching more funky, way out-of-the-box social studies classes: History of Rock 'n Roll, Social

History of Chocolate, Gilded Age in America, Strange and Eccentric People, Black Plague, and my personal favorite: Billy Joel's We Didn't Start the Fire: A Cold War History of the U.S. I would wander the shelves in the library and see what subject spoke to me to teach that semester.

Prior to having kids, I was a high school guidance counselor. I have always loved working with teens, as I think they see the world in a unique way and are at the cusp of learning societal conventions. I loved teaching the classes to them because we could have these great discussions and they were always open to questioning why things are the way they are. They did not just assume that things had always been this way; they were willing to entertain the possibility that things could be different. I cherish that. I would never last in an institutional setting because I love the opportunity to share my own opinions about why things are the way they are, and my opinions are generally fairly irreverent!

As I developed more confidence in our homeschooling journey, I reached out to the community, offering support to others in similar situations. Three friends and I started a gifted homeschool support group for families with gifted children, which met monthly. We encouraged others who were starting out with homeschooling, or having doubts. Sharing our stories and offering resources helped everyone.

I was certainly the most "unschooling"-oriented of us all, and over time, became known as such throughout the homeschool community. Unschooling is a homeschooling approach which follows the child's lead. There is a range of practices within this approach. While we certainly used some curriculum along the way, more and more, I have seen that the principles of following the child's lead and timeframe work. I liken it to toilet training. You can spend years or you can spend days—the end result is the same, and you can have needlessly stressed your relationship with your child for no reason.

Now, homeschoolers throughout the area know that I am a resource for all things unschooling. I encourage people to trust their own instincts, for to me, that is the bottom line of it all.

Having profoundly gifted children has been an amazing gift. I discovered long ago that our lives would not be "normal" according to societal standards. In order to meet the needs of my children, I would have to think outside the box on a daily basis. I could not assume a standard approach and at the same time, honor who they are. Todd had a much harder time accepting that our lives would not be based on a boilerplate. I, however, embrace the differences and celebrate them. Todd has come around in time, but I think he still mourns that part which could fit in more easily. I am happy to make my own way, encouraging others that they can too.

I was blessed early on in discovering the profoundly gifted (pg) community. This network of people around the country has been such a gift to me, empowering my choices and encouraging me to follow my own instincts. Since Adam was two years old, I have been part of various online pg communities, and since he was seven years old, an in-person community each summer. While this group has been wonderful for my children, it has meant even more to me. Everyone needs a place to belong; I have found my people. Each family in this community is unique in its own way, many as outside-the-box as me. I feel at home being different.

Years ago, I began exploring a healthier lifestyle. Again, prompted by Adam, I investigated and researched nutritional differences we could make in our lives: a bit outside the norm societally, but not too dramatically. We have maintained that direction while not being nearly as radical as many of my friends. Different levels of observance work for different families. At a homeschool function once several years ago, I was teased that I couldn't even fit in with a group of homeschoolers (every society has their norms, and I was even bucking those). Again, trust your own instincts to know what is right for you.

Trusting your own instincts is where this post applies to everyone. So for those of you reading for whom the homeschooling part wasn't relevant...here is where it is relevant for your life too. I thoroughly and firmly believe that we all know what is right for us; we just need to trust in our own instincts rather than listening to societal conventions. I have never embraced societal conventions, and in fact, loved utopian novels when I was younger because they showed many different ways of being outside the norm.

If you think you do not know what the right choice for you is, flip a coin. Not to let the coin flip decide, but because once the coin is in the air, you will know your heart's desire.

People do know what is right for them; they are just often not sure enough of their own rightness that they are willing to act. They are constrained by "shoulds," by guilt, by what people will think.

I had the good fortune to have dinner with a dear friend from college about two months ago. In discussing the choices I had made over the prior several months, I said that I felt no regrets, no wavering, about moving out. He laughed and said, "Of course not, why would you? You have always been a person who figured it all out in your head first, and then acted. So why would you ever second-guess yourself? You already know the right path before you act." What an empowering statement.

I will write more later about a book I just finished reading about a month ago, but there is one passage which is particularly applicable here. The book is *Five Secrets You Must Discover Before You Die*, by John Izzo. It is a powerfully wonderful book. Its second secret is "Leave no Regrets." The author found that people who had lived good lives found that *not* doing something is infinitely worse than doing it and having it turn out poorly. Always venture; do not wish for what might have been.

I am now reading a wonderful book called *Steering by Starlight* by Martha Beck. She describes a feeling in your body of "shackles on" versus "shackles off." It is the sense of knowing the freedom of the right choice, fully and bodily. Most people do not honor the feeling; they simply go on with the choices they have been making without question.

Many people go through life unconsciously, following societal conventions without question. I was given a gift months ago to begin to question. I have no doubt in my mind—none—that all that was leading up to all this. Of course, when faced with a serious illness, one's perspective changes. It would have changed now regardless, but I was given the gift of clarity months ago, and I continue to clarify each day. Everything in my life has been developing exactly as it was meant to in order to make this challenge the least disruptive for my children. Todd has developed an amazing relationship with them that has allowed me to take a back seat right now, when I must. I have been disengaging from being completely enmeshed in their lives, and that has allowed all this to be as easy as possible for all of us.

I am incredibly thankful for all of my family and friends who have stepped up to help make this as good as it can be for my children. Friends who have taken them for playdates to their homes (without me, which they have almost never done!), friends far and wide who have offered to Skype to teach them anything they'd like, my parents, and Todd. They have all allowed me to step back and focus on getting well, while knowing that it is the many communities that I have built, both intentionally and by happy accident, that will continue to sustain us all.

I have been incredibly touched by the people reaching out to share their homeschooling stories with me; people who tell me the influence I have had on their philosophy with their children, and most especially, the confidence they have in themselves. To me, that is the most valuable gift I can give: the empowerment of trusting in your own instincts. Each of us knows our own true path: honor yours and follow it.

December 27

Goodbye, Hair...

I went to get my wig on Thursday, December 23. My hair had started to fall out on Monday, and while I still had plenty of hair left, I decided to just get the wig done because the shop would be closed all of Christmas week, and I knew that by New Year's, I would have little hair left.

I am glad I went when I did. The shop owner was amazing and pointed out how much more in control of the situation I was choosing to be, rather than just letting it happen to me. My hair had thinned so much, and I had steroid moon face, so I felt like a chubby little face surrounded by not much hair; I didn't look like me. The wig is fuller and compensates nicely for my fuller face, so I feel much better now.

That morning, I had intended to take a "last picture" of the old hair with the kids. Evan was first. He said he didn't think we should take the picture because it would make me sad and I would just want to forget the time. So we could take it, but then delete it soon. Derek was next, and he definitely wanted a picture. He is the one having the hardest time with the hair.

That morning, taking a shower, was the hardest for me. As I was shampooing my hair, I couldn't help thinking this was the last time I'd be doing it for months. Same thing as I dried my hair. I tried to remember the feeling of my hair as it ran through my fingers.

It was the same feeling as when Derek was two years old and he used to pat my shoulder as I held him and patted his. I said at the time that I wished there was a camera for touch, just as there is a video camera, so that I could always remember how his hand felt as it patted my shoulder. But as soon as I said it, I knew I had burned the sensation in my brain, and would hold that feeling. I have, and can still feel his fingers on me.

My two dear friends, Betty and Ellen, with whom I had dinner that night at the Thai restaurant, came with me to get my wig. I am grateful for their comfort and their friendship, walking beside me every step of the way. They took me to my radiation treatment that morning. Then we had a lovely ladies' lunch al fresco during which Betty finished knitting a fun cap for me, and after, we headed over to the wig shop.

Instead of tears or sadness, we laughed together. The stylist told us what an incredibly different experience it is when a woman is able to go through the experience with friends rather than alone. I am grateful to have had this "playdate" with my dear friends!

The stylist shaved the rest of my hair off and we gathered it in a bag. Thankfully, we found no stray birthmarks or other oddities on my scalp. In fact, the stylist said my head was beautifully shaped and I looked great!

I love the color and the style of the wig; it makes me feel like me.

When I came home, Derek was there to open the door. The wig looked windblown, and he said he didn't like it. I went in and fixed it up, and he was still uncomfortable, but was dealing with it better. Evan saw it next; he asked if that was the wig and said it really didn't look very different. Adam and Todd came home from the gym; Adam didn't even notice until Todd asked, "Oh, did you get your wig today?" And I pointed to my head that yes, I was wearing it. Jaron didn't say anything until hours later, just before bed, when he asked, "Oh, I wonder what you'll look like when you have your wig?" When I said that was my wig, he was so surprised!

I told the kids I would not wear it all the time; it is just too hot, but that I would always wear a hat or scarf or something and not freak them out. As I got ready for bed, I switched to the cap Betty had given me until I was ready to lie down and close my door.

It felt strange to lie on the pillow! It felt like Velcro, kind of spiky, with lots of friction. You don't realize how much hair smoothes your turning your head on a chair or pillow! They did shave off the hair, but it really just looks, and feels, like a buzz cut right now, as the follicles have not fallen out yet. In time, it will just be scalp, which I hope by then, won't bother me as much. The buzz cut is kind of a nice transition; it actually feels kind of good to rub!

On Friday, I went to the store to buy some hats. It was, of course, my first time out without hair. I did not feel like wearing the wig; I just wore a Pokémon baseball cap, so you could tell I had no hair. A wonderfully kind woman who worked at the store followed me out the door after I bought the hats. She shared her story, that she was a cancer survivor who had been given no time, and she was five years out. She said she believes she was spared to help others and reach out to share her inspiration with them. She was indeed an inspiration and I felt warmed by her reaching out.

Everyone is away on a cruise until after New Year's, so it is just my mom and me at the house. It will give me ten days to get used to my new head, get some hats and not feel compelled to wear the wig every day around the house.

I am looking forward to friends visiting, a Girls' Night In with a delicious dinner prepared by the daughter of one of my dear friends, along with a chick flick for fun, and just some R&R in a quiet house.

Today, I started my second round of chemo. I wore my wig, and the nurses all asked if I had my hair done over the weekend. They were amazed it was the wig; I am glad it looks so natural! It felt totally comfortable the whole day, so I will have no trouble wearing it out and about.

I enjoyed many delightful hours of conversation with a wonderful friend whom I have known for years through homeschool coops. He teaches, and he taught my kids for a week one summer, years ago. We had always enjoyed our snippets of conversation, but it was such a neat experience to talk for hours about philosophy and life; just such an enjoyable day. I am grateful to him for choosing to spend the day with me, getting to know each other better.

While the kids are away, I have been spending quiet evenings watching Netflix on my computer. (Thank you to my wonderful PGR friends in California for the subscription!) I will let you all know if I have any good recommendations.

December 31

Happy 2011!

I had written a post about personal responsibility, and will share that one later next week. But that is not what today is about. Today is about looking forward into the new year, the new decade, with hope, joy and optimism.

First, a medical update; then, the real message.

Yesterday, I had a very difficult day—a great deal of pain. I had to postpone my treatment appointment until the afternoon, as I just could not get out of bed. I have thankfully only had two really bad days, both this past week when the kids have been away. I will share the graphicness of it for two reasons: first, because my kids and I have shared this graphic description, and they appreciate its vividness (and it's a great history lesson!), and second, because I do not want anyone to think that I am just in denial and ignoring the reality of the situation. I am choosing to focus on the positive, not the pain, though, and that is the key.

So, the pain is like this: Attila the Hun used to kill his enemies by stretching them apart. It felt like Attila was stretching my ankle bones apart. The pain continued through my knees and hands. It eased with ice and eventually, four Vicodin. But I could not move my legs to get out of bed until 11 a.m. It is actually more a side effect of the steroids than the chemo; the doctor described it as, in essence, severe arthritis. If they can ease me off the steroids, I should experience it less.

I went to my radiation treatment in the early afternoon, and was feeling pretty down. My rock, Betty, drove me. She and I have been having wonderful therapy sessions, where I get out all the bad stuff and then, by the end of the conversation, all is joy and light. But we do get through the bad stuff too. On the ride to treatment, we got through all the bad stuff, so I knew the conversation home would be good.

I saw the doctor, and he told me that he had not yet seen the CT scan they did the previous day, but that we could look at it together before I left. He gave me some tips to cope with the pain, and lots of encouragement about dealing with negative, or even just practical doctors, like the one I had encountered at Moffitt when we went for the second opinion. And then, he brought me back to the room with my CT on the screen.

There was an image with a few small x's. He then showed me the original image—a huge red circle encompassing almost the whole screen. The tumor in the lung had shrunken so dramatically, it almost could not be seen. I felt like Scrooge when he came back from Christmas future! As I left the office, I just wanted to dance and skip and run. My kneecap hurt, so I was only able to hobble, but inside, I was jumping for joy!

The doctor had told me how dramatically the tumor in the lung would shrink with the chemo and radiation. Small cell lung cancer is so deadly because it grows so rapidly that it generally metastasizes before they ever find it in the lung, which is exactly what happened to me. Because of the rapidity of the growth, it is particularly amenable to treatment, which is why it shrinks so dramatically.

I will have an MRI of my brain again next week to see how stable those metastases are. The hope has been that enough of the chemo will travel through the blood/brain barrier (which has already established a pathway through the metastases) that it will either shrink the lesions or at least allow stability so that they could attack the primary tumor first and hopefully prevent further spread. I have not had worsening neurological symptoms, so the MRI next week will hopefully confirm good news in my brain as well.

I was diagnosed on December 1, began treatment on December 6, and have now finished two rounds of chemo and four weeks of radiation to my lung. The plan is for me to have two more weeks of lung radiation, two more rounds of chemo, and then radiation to my brain. Following that course of standard treatment, I will hopefully enter the clinical trial at Moffitt and go forward from there. Take each day as it comes, for truly, each day is a gift.

Which is the real message of this post.

Something Extraordinary

The last day of the year generally sparks reflection and insight for many people. As one looks back upon the year past and forward to the one upcoming, one thinks of what to do differently, what has worked, what to change. I am not doing anything differently, perhaps simply more dramatically.

I have been in this reflection phase for quite a while now—months—and the insights keeps coming every day. I have been incredibly blessed by this gift of clarity, this gift of others sharing their lives with me in a way people just generally don't.

There is something about a cancer diagnosis that allows people to talk to you, to open up and share ideas and changes they have made in their own lives.

Here are some tips for living that I would like to pass on that people have kindly and generously shared:

1. Pick up the tab for the person behind you in the drive-through. While this has gone well almost exclusively, one person was upset and said, "I can pay for my own meal!" The answer? "Of course you can; pay it forward and pay for the guy behind you."

2. When cut off in traffic, bless and love the person: "I love you. Thank you for helping me be alert in my driving today." This will lower your blood pressure and make you a kinder, gentler driver.

3. Be a good phone daughter or son. If your relationship

in person with your parent isn't always the easiest, at least make it okay on the phone. It's often easier.

4. Give more to the world than you take. Whether it be through service, words, or anything else, give more than you take.

5. You can choose with whom you spend your time and the words from them that you allow to enter into you. If someone's words are distressing to you, you can ask them to stop speaking those words, and choose to walk away.

6. We live in an amazing country. The media tries to scare us into thinking everything is terrible, but the reality is that we live in technological marvel and better creature comfort than 90 percent of the rest of the world.

7. Share resources. Both the *CaringBridge* and *Lotsa Helping Hands* websites have now been shared around the country, to help a multitude of others who are sharing difficult circumstances: an easy way to ease burdens, thanks to technology.

8. Help others make connections. This is something I have always loved to do, and I am thrilled each time I see it happening. A friend who brought me for treatment may now tutor the granddaughter of one of my nurses. Who knows the influence he may have on her life? I met a new friend who drove over an hour to take me to treatment because we have mutual friends who felt we should meet. I have many friends for whom I have made connections

who are now special people in each other's lives. Look for what connects you to those you know and help them find it in each other.

9. Make time for others. I was lucky to have reached out to others I had not seen in a long while before I was diagnosed. I was able to see many of these friends for dinner, breakfast and at parties. Now, many more have reached out and are driving me to my appointments, as well as sending wonderful words online.

10. Build a community. Reach out now and establish the support. Whether you ever need it or not, you will always have it. And it will only enrich your life.

11. Share your story. Reach out to people. The woman who came out and shared her survival story (which lots of people are doing, and I love!) touched me. You can touch people easily.

12. Tell people what they mean to you and have meant to you, qualities you see in them. I have made it a point each day to give back the gift everyone has given so generously to me. The profound impact people have made on me by telling me the impact I have had on them, I am doing the same back. It matters to people, and is a gift few people receive.

13. Reach out to family you may not have seen in years. I have connected with a cousin in a whole new way. Is it too little, too late? No, there is always time to establish a

relationship with someone, and family is an easy place to start.

14. Listen to the Universe. I had no idea a year ago what 2010 would bring. I was in Georgia at this time last year. We were at the Georgia Marathon, a Pokémon tournament in which you can play a Cities event every day for ten days. We played for five, had an amazing time, and met people from all over the country. From the very first day of 2010, things changed for me. 2010 brought more changes, insights and growth in my life than any other time since childhood. Everything was connected and everything made sense. My life continues to evolve.

May 2011 bring great health, joy, hope and love to all.

Something Extraordinary

January 7, 2011

This week brought great news and challenges, but heck, it's all good.

First, the great news, which is what did come first. I had the follow-up MRI of my brain, which showed a remarkable 40 percent improvement! This is just from the chemo treatment, as there has been no radiation to my brain (unlike my lung, which has had both). The swelling has gone down enough that my doctor took me off the anti-seizure medication and agreed to the reduction of the steroid from three times a day to twice a day. This, in turn, has removed the side effect of the joint pain (the Attila pain), for which I am ever so grateful!

And I *love* that my doctors chose this course of action. When we went for the second opinion at Moffitt Cancer Center, the doctor there said his course of treatment would have been radiation to the brain first, which is standard therapy. But my doctors wanted to treat my disease as limited (just the lung) even though it had spread to the brain because they felt confident the chemo would address the brain as well.

I have two oncologists, both of whom are terrific. The one who manages the radiation is a world-class doctor who is up on all the latest research throughout the world. He travels to NIH in Maryland every week to stay current and is very knowledgeable about every study. Together, the two doctors (the other manages the chemo part) suggested this plan of action to which I agreed. This will allow me to save much more of my healthy brain tissue.

I feel like a maverick stallion running free from the herd, beating the Moffitt guys' ideas. Gee, do you think that the part of me that bucks societal convention may be coming out a bit?

The challenging part of the week came later that same day. I started to not feel well (mainly chills) and took my temperature. It was 100.1 degrees. I called the doctor and when he called back, I took it again. It was 100.5, which is the point at which I was supposed to go to the hospital. He called in prescriptions for two antibiotics and told me to try those, but if I felt worse during the night, to call him back and he would probably admit me.

Background explanation: I had received chemo the week before, and seven to ten days following chemo, your blood counts generally drop. After the first round, they remained strong, even increased. But this time, that wasn't the case.

I didn't feel worse during the night, and in fact, ate breakfast the next morning. But during the car ride to the center for radiation treatment, I started to get more tired and couldn't really talk, just listen. I kept my eyes closed and rested. When the nurses brought me in to check my blood counts, they were shocked—the white blood cell count was disturbingly low. My temperature was 102.5. The doctor said they would need to admit me to the

Something Extraordinary

hospital, but would infuse me with antibiotics and fluids at the center first to ensure it was done quickly.

They set me up with the IV antibiotics and waited. My temperature came down, and after about two hours, I asked if they could call my friend who had driven me to bring me some lunch because I was hungry. "She's hungry!" the nurse shouted. All the nurses offered to share their lunches with me. The other patients in the chemo room offered to share whatever they had as well.

Everyone said, "Wow! She turned a corner! She looks so much better!" It was like having my own cheerleading squad. It was very uplifting as each patient encouraged me. Throughout the day, as they left, they each came over and said what a difference from how I looked when I walked in.

By the end of the infusion of four different antibiotics and two liters of saline, my temperature was normal and my blood pressure acceptable. The nurse gave me a shot of Neulastin, a medicine to help build white blood cells quickly. When I asked if it would hurt, she said it might give me bone pain, as it was stimulating the bone marrow, and may press against the bone. When I remarked the next day that it hadn't hurt at all, she explained that was probably because my marrow was so depleted, that there was plenty of room for the white blood cells to grow, so no pain!

The doctor said there was no need to go to the hospital at

that point because all the IV antibiotics were to be given just once a day anyway, so there was nothing different they would do there than if I just went home. So I could and I did. Being in a hospital, even in isolation, is the worst thing when you have no immune system, because of all the bizarre bacteria there. So I escaped!

I went back to the center the next day and the counts were still terribly low, but I had no fever. They again infused me with the antibiotics and saline and gave me the shot. It was so much better than having to go to the hospital.

It all turned out fine. Infection had been my biggest fear because it sounded very scary to not be able to fight off anything. But I experienced it and beat it—as I will this whole thing. All good.

A delightful side benefit of being confined to my room has been that Derek has been visiting me each night after dinner to talk. When the boys came back from the cruise they had been on with Todd, they were all sick except Derek, who had been sick before they left. As a result, he is the only one who can be near me, but that is who he is anyway—he loves to talk about real things. Derek is an old soul. He has blown me away by his depth of understanding and insight since he was two years old.

Several months ago, he came to me one morning and shared how happy he was when he woke up that morning. He was pleasantly surprised to find himself hugging his favorite stuffed animal, his puffin. "It was so nice waking up with someone you love in your arms."

He was the one who most clearly expressed his upset when I moved out. But he also was the one who talked about it the most. From the very first day, when he did his own therapy through Puffin, telling me how he felt and then when it got too hard, speaking through Puffin and completely expressing his thoughts and emotions, I knew he'd be okay because he could talk about anything. He has always been incredibly expressive and intuitive.

Last night's topics of conversations, over an hour's time, ranged as follows:

1. Explanation of the different components of blood, and why the white blood cells were so important.

2. When he commented that cancer was a hard thing to have to go through, I commented that it was all part of shaping who you are. That even the things that may seem bad initially all shape who you are and who you become, so while something may seem difficult or even a negative experience when you are going through it, none of it is, because it all shapes who you become. And you can choose to look at it positively in helping shape you.

3. He had been complaining a few nights earlier that he found it difficult to sleep in the same room with Evan, who was snoring because he was sick. I suggested he consider sleeping in an extra bed in a separate room.

He told me then that he had not, that he had chosen to sleep in his own bed each night, because he was afraid of ghosts at night. He said he doesn't really believe in them during the day, but at night, your mind thinks differently about things.

4. He thanked me on Puffin's behalf, saying how grateful she was for all I had done for her since she came to live with us, and how she could never repay me all my kindness. I thanked him and told him that anything I ever did for her I did out of love and that anything I do for anyone, person or puffin, comes from choosing to do it, or just being who I am, never with the expectation of repayment. And I told him about Paying it Forward. That was the greatest way Puffin could ever thank me, because if we can pay it forward and help others through the kindness we have received, it will only serve to make the world a better place.

5. He came up with a motto to print on the money issued in Puffin Land by Puffin: "Any day with a Puffin, or Anyone You Love, is a Good Day."

6. Denominations of money, including the largest currency ever issued by the U.S. and the currency of other countries. Talked about why different countries may have larger denominations than the U.S. and how their economies differ.

7. Why countries can't just print more money indefinitely to give people more money.

8. He wondered why "rich people aren't as nice as poor people," which prompted a discussion of material wealth and focus on things versus focus on people and relationships, and while there are certainly exceptions to that concept, perhaps people who have less focus more on each other. This was the case with the happiness survey of the major countries, which showed Mexico as one of the happiest countries, presumably because of the focus on relationships rather than stuff.

9. He commented that he couldn't wait until there was no more money and people would use barter and trade instead. He said it was a shame people had to have money to buy the things they wanted. We talked about how more people are bartering now because they do have less money, and how it was easier to barter with an individual for a service than a company for an object. He suggested you could trade in your object for something different; again, why this was easier with an individual, but some stores may work that way too.

10. We spoke of how money began when early man used it to make trades more fair. He thought that the system of trade and barter would be more fair, particularly to those who didn't have much.

11. Habitat for Humanity—I told him of this organization that my dad and I had volunteered for a few years ago and that I continue to support, as it does truly help people who are willing to help themselves, and I believe it does good work.

12. He told me of a commercial he had seen repeatedly on the cruise, which spoke of rebuilding homes in Haiti. How poor the infrastructure had been there and why so many people died and lost their homes. How strong was the Haiti earthquake?

13. Looking up online how strong the strongest earthquakes were and finding out that four of the strongest ten were in Indonesia. Why? Ring of Fire. How many people died in those earthquakes versus other strongest ones in Alaska and Siberia—so few lives affected there. Why people choose to live where they do.

This is my eight-year-old child. I am so blessed. There is great hope in the world.

January 12

Let It Go, Let It Go, Let It Go

In *Steering By Starlight*, Martha Beck relates the following story about her autistic son, Adam:

> He received a new watch for Christmas that year and he was very proud of it. The first day back at school after the holiday, a classmate borrowed Adam's watch, dropped it and broke it. The teacher was horrified.
>
> "Jared!" she exclaimed to the watch-breaker. "You should have been more careful! That was Adam's watch!"
>
> All day, the teacher felt horrible about her part in the watch-breaking incident. Her mind spun out long stories about how irresponsible she'd been to let Jared borrow the watch, how she should have known better, how Adam was suffering and how angry his mother would be. She dealt with her own guilt and shame by repeatedly scolding Jared for the entire day. The next day, she raised the subject again. Later, while the class was working on a project, Adam approached her desk.
>
> "Ms. Morrison," he politely observed. "It was my watch."

"I know, honey," Ms. Morrison groaned, feeling just awful. "I shouldn't have let you lend it to Jared."

"No," said Adam, frowning in frustration. "It was my watch."

"And it was awful that he broke it. I'm so sorry."

Adam began to laugh. Then, for several seconds, he thought very hard, the way he does when he absolutely has to make himself understood.

"Ms. Morrison," he said very slowly, "it...was...my...watch. Not...yours." He looked at her intently to see if she'd get it. And then, for Ms. Morrison, the light dawned.

"Oh," she said. "You mean, I should let it go?"

Adam burst out laughing again, heaved a huge sigh of relief, and went back to his seat.

Another part of the lesson to let it go comes from the second of *The Four Agreements* by Don Miguel Ruiz:

> *"Don't Take Anything Personally: Nothing others do is because of you. What others say and do is a projection of their own reality, their own dream. When you are immune to the opinions and actions of others, you won't be the victim of needless suffering."*

I have been struck by how some people have reacted to my news. Some take on the burden: "I am so saddened. I am so shocked." I understand and appreciate, and I know that sometimes, there are no words to say, or that words pour out in sympathy. I just want people to not take this on themselves. Of course it is not something I would choose, but I am looking at it in such a positive way, that it is but a part of the journey. Please do not feel sorry for me or think how terrible life is…it is not. It is beautiful.

It was similar when I told people I was moving out. I know everyone has their own issues, and I fully understand that some people are facing their own situations and could not possibly be supportive of mine. But they took it personally, as if it was about them. How my marriage has anything to do with anyone aside from Todd and me, I just cannot imagine. Some people recognized that my choices were my choices, and were wonderfully supportive.

At the time, I consciously chose those to whom I would reach out. I created a supportive network of friends who have continued to be there for me throughout. And I distanced myself from those who, for various reasons, could not offer support. I did not do this judgmentally but practically. And now that I am facing a different set of challenges, I continue to appreciate the support of those who are reaching out now as well as those who were there for me then. I have made a conscious effort to consider other people's point of view and how things affect them. I have tried to understand their position and why things may affect them in certain ways, considering their position instead of thinking of my own.

I need to be in a good place, and choose with whom I spend my time: those who enrich and nurture me, not those who bring me down in any way. I am choosing love, light, joy, happiness, peace, and moving forward, and need those enriching, nurturing people around me, supporting my journey.

One of the issues to which I think some of this relates is that of personal responsibility. It amounts to nothing more than being responsible for your own stuff, and your stuff only. I have always tried to instill this in my children as well. They have been responsible for their own laundry for years. It is not just a matter of washing the clothes (Derek and Evan can't reach the controls easily, so I help them); it is the mental piece of knowing when the laundry must be done. It is a matter of bearing the mental load of knowing they are about to run out of clothes and that they need to do something about the situation. It is not my responsibility to ask if they have plenty of clean clothes left.

Similarly, I fully appreciate everyone's support and outpouring of love when I was diagnosed. The mental piece of dealing with cancer is mine. As for the support of dealing with it (rides to appointments, meals, great conversations, messages and support), I welcome help from everyone around me.

Control is a large piece of the puzzle too. When I was a kid, my dad framed and hung the Serenity Prayer on the basement wall. I saw it almost every day from the time I was probably six or seven years old:

> *God grant me the serenity*
> *to accept the things I cannot change;*
> *courage to change the things I can;*
> *and wisdom to know the difference.*

I don't know that I consciously chose to live my life that way, but looking back now, this prayer surely influenced me, and I incorporated it into my life.

Knowing when to just accept a situation is huge. I do not try to control things anymore; I accept all and change what I can. And a large part of that is other people. I have no control whatsoever over another person's actions, only over my own and my own reactions. When people don't feel they have control in their own lives, they seek a place in which they can feel power and control. And if that means in someone else's life, it is obtrusive as well as unproductive, because, of course, you can only change yourself.

I have let so much go. I am blessed to be relieved of much responsibility because, between Todd and my mother, the lion's share of taking care of the kids has been lifted from me. And, as I said, I have always taught my kids to be self-reliant and independent, and have been disentangling from their lives for months now. But little mental things—so many details that are just truly unnecessary, are gone. The beautiful part for me is that it is not even an effort; it has come naturally to me as I am able to focus on what is important and let the rest go, completely.

There are dozens of decisions we each make every day that really do not matter at all in the great scheme of life. Should I eat my pie with a fork or a spoon? Should I store the salad in a bag or in a bowl? Should I bring out the garbage at night or in the morning? Small, inconsequential decisions that waste our energy are completely off my radar. I have no opinion about the small things like this that just don't matter. I expend no mental energy on decisions that are not important. I am putting my energies where they do matter: helping my kids chart their paths, helping others with their journeys, helping myself get well.

There is a Zen-like feeling when you do this. You watch the world go by and only choose to engage with certain pieces. It is a very freeing feeling to know you do not need to have an opinion about everything. Conscious choices, conscious non-choices, conscious detachment and conscious engagement, we are free to partake in all. I have found great calm in letting go.

January 18

Monks and Medical Update

In Tibet, when a Buddhist monk is in training, he is dependent on his surrounding community. He goes door-to-door for his food, and every member of the community invites him to share their meals. They know that he is representing them in his journey, and they sustain his odyssey. He, in turn, meditates and discovers profound truths that he later shares with the community.

I have never been a gourmand. I eat because I need to fuel my body. With the kind and generous outpouring of my friends to sustain my family during this time, I feel like a Tibetan monk, except I do not need to go door-to-door; the community is coming to me. I am so grateful to everyone who has offered sustenance to my family. You all have introduced new tastes to us, while kindly following our requests for simple meals. We look forward to what surprise greets us at dinnertime!

I began my third round of chemo yesterday. I am halfway done with my chemo/radiation treatment, which is hard to believe because it all still seems new to me, like I have just begun, yet the end of traditional treatment is in sight.

Because my brain scan had been fairly clear, my doctor lowered my dose of the steroids which had been causing me many problems. However, after just a few days without the higher dose, I began having balance problems again, I was walking with a drift, my eyes and ears just weren't clear, and I felt as I had felt back in October before I knew what was wrong. When I told my doctor, he said, "Well, we tried," and put me back on the higher dose of steroids. This time, they are not bothering me quite as much.

He also told me that we would begin radiation to my brain immediately following the conclusion of radiation to my lung. So next week, I begin brain radiation. He again assured me, "You won't get stupid." It is a scary thought. He did say I may lose some executive function—I may not be able to find words as easily. When I shared that caveat with my brother, he said, "I can't find words all the time too! It's just part of getting older."

My legs, which had been bothering me very much, are better now, thanks to a marvelous physical therapy session. The man who has been Adam's trainer for years is an incredibly spiritual person who can do just about anything to heal the body. He stretched my legs, taught me how to re-train the muscles, and then had me walk. I was shuffling my legs and he reminded me, "Swing your arms!" I had forgotten how to walk in such a short time because I had been fearful of falling. This small change completely changed my gait and gave me back my confidence.

Now I stride easily with legs that don't hurt as much. They are getting stronger as I force the muscles to do what they should rather than lift my legs with my hands. This change has carried through to the rest of my body as I stand straighter and feel more upbeat.

I did find out that I will be unable to drive, indefinitely. This knowledge has changed my thoughts and plans for the immediate future as I realize that, going back to that Tibetan monk, I will be dependent on my community for a lot longer than I thought. I am totally fine with that. I have absolutely no desire to drive; I am grateful for the help and support of others and have no problem continuing to reach out to others to help me at this point in my journey. There is a time to be independent and a time to rely on others. Now is my time for reliance, so I am asking for everyone's help to allow me to continue to live my life, just with a little bit of extra help!

January 20

Every Day Is a Gift

No one knows how much time he has on this Earth. Accidents happen every day, surprise diagnoses await us. Everyone is walking on the edge of a cliff covered by a bank of fog. One just does not know that one is walking on the edge. Some of us have been gifted with the knowledge that life is short and we do not know when that end will come: the fog has lifted off that cliff. We see clearly the edge of the cliff and know that we are all walking perilously on the edge...

I entitled my blog page "Each Day Is A Gift." It is absolutely clear to me more and more each day how much this is true. But I have always tried to live my life this way, although I must admit that I have often failed. There had been days that I just got by, or was not looking forward to, or could not wait to end so I could try again the next day.

When the kids were younger, if we had a particularly difficult day, I did try to be conscious of the fact that the day was not over until it was over. Instead of just rushing to bed to relieve the pressure of the day, I was proud if I remembered to "Redeem the day." A simple thing like a quiet bath for them before bed would ease away the tension of the day, and we would all be able to go to bed with a happy memory instead of the difficulty of the day.

In *Five Secrets You Must Discover Before You Die*, the fourth secret is "Live the Moment." This is about focusing on the here and now, and it is also about never just "getting through" a day. There is always something important to be found in each day, even if you feel you are doing exactly the same thing you did yesterday. Find at least one thing to celebrate each day, one thing to remember, to be grateful for, to do differently, to make that day unique.

In his famous speech, "Don't Give Up, Don't Ever Give Up," after he was diagnosed with cancer and knew he had a short time to live, Coach Jim Valvano shared his secrets to living a fulfilling life.

> "To me, there are three things we all should do every day. We should do this every day of our lives. Number one is laugh. You should laugh every day. Number two is think. You should spend some time in thought. Number three is, you should have your emotions moved to tears, could be happiness or joy. But think about it. If you laugh, you think, and you cry, that's a full day. That's a heck of a day. You do that seven days a week, you're going to have something special."

Imagine that simple formula. How many of us are actually moved to such a strong emotion every day? How many of us walk through life in that fog, never fully engaging in our emotions? Toddlers laugh, on average, 400 times each day; by the time we are adults, we are lucky if we laugh, truly laugh, a dozen times a day. And tears? When is the last time you were moved to tears? Either because you were laughing so hard or because something moved you that deeply? Or because of deep sadness?

Last week, a friend who drove me to treatment was telling me stories of her travels. They were hysterical and I was belly laughing; what a gift to be able to laugh like that! I want to do it more, every day. But I also appreciate those friends who are more temperate. That is my nature. I have had the pleasure of being back in touch with my best friend from when I was 14. She reminded me that when she and another friend from then "freaked out," I was always the one to bring them back to center. I have always been the calming influence with my friends and family. So I certainly appreciate moderation as well, but sometimes, those extreme emotions have their place too.

There is nothing wrong with experiencing the full range of emotion; we need to do so. People are so afraid of being sad or upset that they block that and cover it up. We need to feel it all, and let our kids know it is okay to feel it all. If we only allow them to be happy, they will never experience the full joy of being human. They will think that they are not acceptable if they are not upbeat. This is particularly difficult for those parents who are extroverts while their kids are introverts. Let them be exactly who they are. They do not need dozens of friends surrounding them; they do not need to have a smile on their face all the time. They are usually perfectly content being exactly who they are, as long as we give them permission.

The same is true for kids who just feel things more deeply. When Jaron was four, he came to my bedroom early one morning in tears. We had spoken the day before about the sun and how much longer it would last—four billion more years. He had woken up at 5 a.m. in tears because he had the revelation that life would not be there forever. Yes, it was four billion years in the future and it would not personally affect him, but the revelation of impermanence was profound. He made the connection that things would not always stay the same. It was not long after that when he was again moved to tears with the realization that he would not always live in the family house: that one day, he would grow up and live on his own.

From a young age, Jaron has always felt more deeply than many. He has been moved to tears by a sunset or a rainbow. To me, this is a beautiful and miraculous gift which I seek to nurture. It gets harder as he gets older, as he is more aware of those darn societal conventions which tell him it is not okay to cry about things like that. We have always spoken about how his highs are higher than most people's, but his lows are also lower. Over the years, he has learned how to deal with his emotions. I hope he will always honor who he is and not squelch his true nature. It will truly be a gift if he is able to be moved to extreme emotion each day; it is a gift for us all.

To be fully present in each moment, sit in the front row of life. Take everything life has to give: every pleasure, every moment fully lived, every rose along the way. Rather than getting through to a destination, appreciate every step along the way.

A key piece of this is not to judge your life. From moment to moment, stop asking yourself, "Am I a success? Am I a failure?" Stop judging and simply live each moment as it comes. Be fully present and engaged, whether you are doing the dishes or having a profound conversation with your loved one. It all matters; it is all important. It all shapes you and contributes to who you are. There are no insignificant moments, despite how it may feel at the time, if we put our full attention to the now.

I must admit this is much more difficult than it sounds. This past summer, I read *The Power of Now* by Eckhardt Tolle, a fantastic book which extols the essential idea to "live in the now." I had absolutely no idea how to do this. I understood intellectually, but was unable to put it into practice, as my thoughts raced and I found it extremely difficult to stop my mind from going to the past and future. Suggestions I have read include meditation first and foremost, which may not be for everyone. There are three other pieces, though, which I think are infinitely doable: first, gratitude. If we are grateful each day for the gifts life has bestowed upon us, it helps us be much more present in the moment. Months ago, I began a gratitude journal in which I write every evening, reminding my subconscious of the joy of the day.

The second practice is to realize that we can consciously choose to look at the positive in each interaction. Yes, we can get just "get through" our day, our work, or we can see the gift in each moment.

Jim Valvano was Italian. He credited much of his zest for life to his heritage. I recently watched two movies, both partially set in Italy: *Only You* and *Eat, Pray, Love*. I was struck by the depiction of how Italians embrace life versus how Americans get through life. In Italy, life is relished: Italians savor their food, spending hours eating and tasting each bite; they take a siesta each day, enjoying their families or an extra few hours alone with a spouse; they cherish the vistas of their extraordinary landscape. In short, they indulge their senses and appreciate the gifts around them. This is a third way to live in the moment: follow your senses. When our senses are fully engaged, we cannot help but be present. Our focus can be nowhere but in our bodies, and that takes us out of our minds and into the moment.

I have been given the gift of being able to live in the now. For me, these tools are helpful, but no longer necessary. It is clear to me how precious each and every moment, each and every day, is. I no longer have to make the effort. Each day, I rejoice in the books I read, the movies I watch, the people with whom I speak, the interactions with those whom I spend the day. I am grateful for all.

January 24

Schooling

Some of you have kindly been concerned about what the plan is for the kids' schooling. While this has certainly been a concern for me as well, it is all in how you view it. As I have pointed out for all of us, everything is a learning experience—everything you experience shapes you.

As a homeschooler, I know that this extends to all of life, including "school" topics, which is how I have taught my children. I briefly explained unschooling in a prior post; the idea is that we are all learning all the time from everything we do. Adam is fond of saying they learn from the air. However, I do recognize that because I am no longer as available to just hang out and be with the kids, that perhaps a bit more formal of a learning plan can be a positive choice at this time.

School was never an option. We are homeschoolers; that is definitely a part of my kids' identity. When we told them I was moving out back in September, their very first question was, "Will we still be homeschooled?" Evan has said he would rather be sent to Antarctica than to school! This is in no way a condemnation of those who choose school; merely an explanation of how integral a part of them homeschooling is. So we started thinking of ways to make it work better for now.

Community was the first thing that came to mind. The point is that you don't need to do everything yourself. I have always been a facilitator in the homeschool journey, finding the best resources that would fulfill the kids' needs. I have a friend I have known for over ten years who has done a remarkable job with her own homeschooled son and is now studying educational consulting. A mutual friend with whom I was discussing my desire for someone to help make a plan for the kids and perhaps work with them a few hours each week, suggested I contact her. We met, she met with the kids, and she will help us develop a plan for them for each week, as well as work with them individually.

I have set up a monthly workshop for the kids and their friends with a wonderful man who teaches amazing classes at homeschool co-ops. He is someone I want my kids to know and spend time with; while the topics he will cover will be fascinating to them, I really just want them to get to know him and learn from him.

This is something I have known but realized yet again: I want my kids to be surrounded by interesting people. What specific information they may learn from them is fairly irrelevant. The relationship is the important part of the equation. I have seen this clearly with Adam and his bridge friends. He has learned about amazing, obscure things from online forums and in-person interactions with fascinating people. Surrounding yourself with captivating people is the best way to learn and grow.

Friends and family have generously reached out to us and offered to Skype with the kids about anything they'd like to learn about. I thank you all! It is very reassuring to know that you are out there as a resource, and as I have said, the topic is irrelevant; the relationship is key.

We are also fortunate enough to have maintained a relationship with the woman who has been the kids' nanny since Derek and Evan were born. While she only came once or twice a month for the past few years, Cathy has been a part of our family all along. She has generously agreed to come back and work for us part-time. She will be in charge of the kids' schooling, but also in further teaching them independence and life skills. She will help the kids cook and maintain the household, just as she did when they were younger, but with much more responsibility on them now that they are older.

Adam is home for six weeks between tournaments, which is very unusual, as he is usually only home for two or three weeks at a time. We were considering an online short college class for him to work on. At two o'clock in the morning, when I was up one night, a flash of insight came to me. I could no longer drive, but as he had just turned 15, he could, as long as I was in the car with him. He could now help with errands, going to Publix, the library, and so on. I approached him with the idea (he previously had no interest in driving yet), and he said he'd be happy to help out. Instead of a random online class, he is now taking Florida Virtual School's driver's ed.

Something Extraordinary

I will still need help from others to drive to appointments and longer distances, and greatly appreciate everyone still supporting me in that regard, but having Adam help with the short-distance runs will help establish a sense of ease and normalcy. The pieces are in place to move forward.

January 27

To Everything, There Is a Season

There are different stages in our lives in which, until you have already made the change to the next one, it is impossible to see or understand someone who is in that next stage.

When you are in the midst of raising your children, particularly when you homeschool, you can see nothing beyond them. At least I could not. I was completely and intimately involved with my kids. I enjoyed being with them all the time and could not imagine a different way of life. I did still have something of a life apart: I would go for a Moms' Night Out once or twice a month, and we would not talk about our kids. I did participate in a book club, but it was with Adam. I saw my friends all the time when we would go to each other's houses, but it was always with the kids.

A friend who has been homeschooling her kids for years had the experience this year of having her kids in school full-time. She recognized that she has now entered a different phase of her life, and can no longer relate to her friends who are fully engaged in homeschooling their kids. She is ready to move on to the next phase of her life, one that concentrates on her more than them.

Another friend gave a wonderful gift to all her homeschooling friends when she hosted a get-together at her house for adults only. Many of the homeschooling moms who attended had rarely been out without their kids. What my friend was trying to do was not only offer these women an outlet to connect with one another, but also to discover or rediscover themselves. She had been through a divorce, and during the process, built an amazing community of friends and established a life for herself that was all based on conscious choices of what she enjoyed spending her time doing. Her message to the other moms was that you do not have to be divorced to do that. You can do this for yourself now, and be a more fulfilled person.

The thing is, when you are in the midst of raising your kids and homeschooling, you are fulfilled. I certainly never felt that I was doing anything above-and-beyond the call of duty. I just liked being around my kids.

So now comes the next part. The kids are still there. The wanting to have them around is still there. But there's more that's needed too. There's a focus and a thought about just me that was never there before. And when you are still in the midst of the other time, the time that I have just now entered seems selfish. It seems like you are too focused on yourself. But you need to be in order to be a whole person. Everyone gets there at some point; many people just wait until their kids are out of the house, and then they have the empty nest and face the loss without having any idea who they are or what direction in which to go because they have always been mom and now have no role to play.

I am just entering that time early. My kids are still here, but I am learning about me now. I love our time together, but I also love our time apart. As I have said, I have always raised them to be self-sufficient, and they are.

I have been able to take the time to discover who I am. Over the summer, I worked with a life coach to help me discover and rediscover. I say discover because while part of the approach to remember what brought you joy in the past and do that again, that is just a piece. I do not feel like ever going back. I only want to move forward. So while what brought me joy in the past may be a clue, I feel like there was a time for that, but that time is done. I have incorporated every part of my past into who I am, but I have absolutely no desire to go back to any of it. I only want to move forward, and choose a new path.

For those who do want to rediscover, talk about what you love. Make lists of what you love to do. Make time to do what you love to do, but if you feel overwhelmed trying to find the time, just talk about it. You will find that it will integrate into your life effortlessly if you talk about it. You will find yourself doing it, or at least moving in that direction. So just talk about it.

Make peace with your past. Accept that whatever happened has shaped you into the person you are now, and you are stronger for it. Rather than judging what was, or what you did, move forward and keep the past in its proper perspective. You cannot change what already happened, so why dwell there?

If your life seemed "better" to you in the past, then you have a different perspective. We can certainly savor the past without regretting that we cannot relive that moment. It can remain a treasured memory, but we can move forward. Many people live in the past, wishing for things to be as they were before, not wanting their kids to grow up, wanting their youth back. It isn't going to happen! Let it go and move forward.

When figuring out what to do next and where to go, you may want to consider advice from John Izzo in *Five Secrets You Must Discover Before You Die*. The second secret is "Leave No Regrets," and one way to do this is to choose the path which makes the best story. One wise elder said this is what he asked himself in making choices, "When I am old and sitting in my rocking chair thinking about my life, what decision will I wish I had made?"

Izzo found that not one person said they regretted having tried something and failed, yet most said they had not taken enough risks. If you are at that time of transition, what is the next step of your journey? What risks will you take that move you out of your comfort zone and into a life you can't yet imagine?

In *Steering By Starlight*, Martha Beck explains the "shackles on" versus "shackles off" feeling, which I have written about before. Beck explains: "If you do nothing more than choose whatever feels most 'shackles off' to you, moment by moment, you will fulfill your best destiny. You will realize your best destiny through the exercise of courage, which means taking whatever action is most liberating to the soul, even when you are afraid."

Living a "shackles off" life brings great integrity, freedom and joy.

January 31

Brain Sizzle

I have begun the next phase of my treatment: brain radiation. The "cage" that surrounds my head during treatment looks like a medieval torture device. I must be totally immobile so that the radiation can be directed to exactly the right part of the brain each time. I can breathe, but cannot swallow, as the mask is quite tight. They crafted it back in December, and my face has swollen more as a result of the steroids, so it is tighter than it was initially, but I did not ask them to re-make it, as it is livable, and it is only for about five minutes or so. It also challenges me to breathe through it. When they place the mask on, I just take deep breaths throughout and stay calm. I enjoy the yogic practice.

One of the side effects of the radiation is fatigue. I have taken two naps each day. Napping is a glorious rejuvenation. I highly recommend it. I have been able to follow my body's rhythms and sleep when I need to. This is the same at night as well. If I wake up at 2 a.m., I do not fight it, but turn on the light and read for an hour or so before I fall back asleep again. It is very nurturing to follow your natural rhythms.

The radiation to my brain feels very interesting. I actually feel like my brain is being cooked. This is a good thing, as that is the goal, but it is indeed an odd sensation. It is only when I lie a certain way that it feels warm inside my head. Not all the time, but enough that I know it's working.

The brain radiation will continue for four weeks, and I have one more round of chemo during that time as well. The end of daily treatment is in sight.

I had the wonderful opportunity to announce the Homeschool Spelling Bee last week. I have run the bee for five years, and back in September, had turned it over to a homeschool friend (in another act of the "everything lining up in anticipation of this life change"), with the caveat that I would still announce. I was very pleased to feel well enough to still participate. It felt wonderful to be a part of the experience after having done it for so many years. I saw old homeschool friends, and enjoyed the banter with the boy who won for the second year. He asked for a definition for each word, and I loved challenging my brain to come up with clever definitions for him. When the word was "panic," my definition was "to freak out." There were "muskrat: a small furry mammal," and "gazelle: a large horned mammal." The bee ran 35 rounds, with 29 rounds of three spellers competing. We made it to the Challenge words for the first time in three years. It was an exciting and true competition.

This past weekend, my college roommate came to visit from Ft. Lauderdale. I really appreciate her coming to spend the time with me. Another college friend who lives in Tampa came as well, and they had not seen each other in 25 years! It was wonderful to catch up, reminisce, and see that we are all facing many similar thoughts at this point in our lives. I am so blessed to have such wonderful dear friends who surround me.

February 3

Leave the World Better Than You Found It

Last week, I had the opportunity to be the announcer for the sixth annual Homeschool Spelling Bee. I have run this bee for the past six years, starting it from scratch when none existed. Adam had competed in a bee the prior year at a part-time school for homeschoolers. He enjoyed the experience, and I wanted to bring that opportunity to him and to others. I looked around the homeschool community, and no one was doing it, so I did.

The same year that Adam had competed in the bee at the school, Jaron had competed in the National Geographic Bee at his Montessori School. They allowed him to compete with the fourth-to-sixth graders even though he was only five years old, and he did terrifically well. The following year, he chose to homeschool, and I wanted him to have the opportunity to compete again in the Bee. So I applied to National Geographic as a homeschool entity, and ran a competition for homeschoolers.

I found that if something did not already exist, or was not already in place, I could either be upset that it wasn't out there and complain that the resources just weren't available, or I could create it myself. I chose to do the latter, over and over again.

When we found that there was not a good resource to support those just beginning their homeschool journeys with their gifted children, three friends and I started a support group. Our group has became a model for support groups in two other counties.

A secular homeschool co-op that I had been involved in was fracturing, as often happens in homeschool groups. So, several friends and I started our own group, which had a fabulous semester with over thirty families enjoying a terrific camaraderie.

How incredibly empowering to know that you can change things for the better. If something does not exist, you can make it happen. Maybe not alone, maybe with a great deal of assistance, but you can make an incredible impact on the world.

The scenarios I have described have been about homeschooling. But of course, this idea applies to many other situations.

For example, my cousin's brother-in-law makes yearly trips to disadvantaged countries, offering free dental services and cleft palate surgeries at his own expense, changing hundreds of lives over the course of a two-week trip.

I have written previously of random acts of kindness—little things that can make an impact, small ways you can change the world. Here is a website that suggests many ideas to try: randomactsofkindness.org.

I have a friend who, whenever he goes to the grocery

store, makes it a point to flirt with the old ladies there. He asks them for advice, or to watch his cart for a moment. What a highlight of their day! In *Mama Gena's School of Womanly Arts*, there is a chapter about flirting, explaining how it is a gift to both the flirter and the flirtee. Really look at the person, see him or her as an individual, and flirt a little. See how it brightens his or her day—and yours!

That is an example of a small thing that you can do each day. But look around for the big stuff too. See what is lacking in your life, in your own community. See if you can change that. Rather than being unhappy with your situation or any perceived lack, try to reach toward abundance. It is out there waiting.

Rather than complaining about your situation, change it. Or at least make a general plan to make it better. Nothing is going to change if you are mired in the same program you have been running all along. Einstein said, "The problems we face cannot be solved at the same level of thinking we were at when we created them." You have to try a creative leap, a new way to address the problem.

This applies to both your own life and the world in general. A definition of suffering: a constant longing for life to be different. If you always want things to be different than they are, you can never be satisfied. If you are not satisfied, find something to change to make things better.

Something Extraordinary

Life is full of opportunities. Find one thing to do differently tomorrow and see how amazing it feels to break out of your routine. It can be so empowering.

February 8

Zen and the Art of Egg Making

As I was making my breakfast this morning, I was struck by the simple yet profound act of making a scrambled egg. Each morning, I get ready for treatment. I prepare my breakfast and sit quietly to eat. Often alone, sometimes with my father or the kids.

For the first month or so after I was diagnosed, my mother prepared my breakfast, as I was just not up to it. When I was finally able to do it myself, it felt like a small triumph, and I have been trying to do it each morning. This small act is empowering. I am grateful that my mother prepares breakfast for the kids and I am able to just focus on my own needs. This is a gift, for focusing only or even mainly on oneself is something that many people are unable to do.

I am able to do this for all of my meals, and have found it to be a lovely respite from responsibility for others. The ability to simply focus on one's own needs is also profound, and something that can transform the way you interact with the world around you. It affords you the ability to be mindful.

Since I began radiation to my brain, I have been a bit frustrated with myself, for I feel unable to think terribly clearly or profoundly. I am much more focused in the moment rather than beyond. But what a gift! The idea of mindfulness, the idea of the "now" rather than the past or the future...that is what people strive for, and it is now just coming naturally to me because of my recent inability to focus beyond the moment. It is such an unusual sensation, since often, our minds race and we inevitably move away from the present.

In her first blog, a friend wrote about spending ten extra minutes preparing oatmeal when she realized that, contrary to the instructions on the box, she preferred the way they tasted when she cooked them a little longer. In the past, she would have just pulled them off the stove at twenty minutes, as the box said, because that is what she was supposed to do. Yet that particular morning, she decided to be kind to herself and prepare the oats the way she wanted, and while 50 percent more time may seem like a lot, what was ten minutes in the grand scheme of life? But the point was that she was choosing to be kind to herself by preparing the food the way that she chose. She was choosing to be mindful about her breakfast, and in doing so, realized a profound truth.

Food can be a brilliant metaphor if we allow it to be. It is not something that ever occurred to me, for as I have mentioned, to me, food is merely sustenance that we must take in. I have never been a gastronome. However, due to the lung radiation, I suffered from esophagitis, a painful swelling of my esophagus, which forced me to eat not only some different, milder foods, but also to eat much more slowly. I would take small bites, chew extensively and often take an hour to eat a salad and sandwich. As I ate this way, I realized this is the ideal way we should eat all the time: slowly, with small bites, mindfully. Most people, especially hurried Americans, eat so quickly that they never even taste their food. Experts say this is a huge contributor to the obesity epidemic.

I, of course, am trying to eat more, as I am trying not just to maintain my weight during treatment, but to regain the twenty pounds I had lost over the past ten months. Since beginning treatment in December, I have actually gained back almost all of it. Some of it is the water weight from the steroids, but much of it is real. The staff is pleased with my gains, for one of the major complications of treatment is weight loss, and I am experiencing exactly the opposite. This helps keep my body strong, not only to fight the cancer but to handle the treatments well. In addition to three meals a day, I snack all the time (which is another way that people should eat—it helps maintain your metabolism).

Today, I spent hours with Lynn, a dear friend whom I have come to know in a whole new way since this journey began. We have known each other for twenty years, and she reminded me today of all the connections we have shared throughout our lives. But despite having known each other for many years, we now share a deep connection that we had not experienced before. We know each other more intimately now, and she has stayed with me every step of the way. I am confident she will remain with me not just through this part of the journey, but afterwards as well. That means the world to me. We shared deep conversation today, so perhaps I am being hard on myself when I conclude that I cannot hold deep thoughts at the moment. Perhaps I can engage them, but the simple thoughts can be fine too. No judging, simply accepting whatever comes. That is the key.

There can be just as much value in thinking these deep thoughts as there can in the simple, peaceful act of cooking a perfect egg.

Adam's Bar Mitzvah, January 2009

With Jaron, six months before my diagnosis

Something Extraordinary

In Hawaii for Pokemon Worlds, August 2010

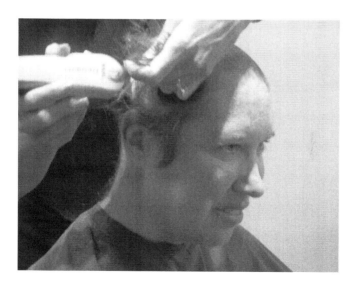

Getting hair shaved off, December 2010

With dear friends Betty and Ellen and my new wig, um, hair

On my 44th birthday, with friends from many years ago

Something Extraordinary

Family tradition: Evan and Derek on bed on their ninth birthday

First vacation after treatment, Williamsburg, VA, Sept. 2011

At Jaron's Bar Mitzvah with dear friend Lynn, Nov. 2011

Chanukah 2011

Reading with my boys, Oct. 2012

All four boys during new chemo treatment, Feb. 2013

February 11

A Tribute to My Parents

My parents have always been there for me. No matter what the circumstance, no matter what happened, they have been behind me.

When Todd first saw the MRI of my brain and realized the seriousness of my condition, whether it was cancer or an infection, he asked if he could call my parents and tell them. I said yes, and they were on a plane within a few hours, arriving the very first evening I went into the hospital. They packed up their life and came immediately, indefinitely, to help in any way they could.

My father went back to Maryland for a few weeks to take care of loose ends and gather more clothes. He plans to stay for a few more months. (In years past, he has stayed with us for a few months each winter, being a snowbird and playing with the kids.) My mother stayed with me all along. She has been my nurse, my and the kids' driver, the cook, the housekeeper, the chief bottle washer.

When she took me to my first chemo treatment, the nurse asked her how she was handling it. My mom answered that she was strong, that she had taken care of her own parents, including her mother through breast cancer. But it was different when it was your child. She took me to pick out the wig that I later picked up with my friends, and took plenty of notes, just as she did when we went to my chemo education, the day before treatment began.

The end of treatment is in sight, less than a month away, and we are winding down for Mom to go back to Maryland. She has done an amazing job of keeping the house running, taking care of the kids and me. She put her life in Maryland on hold and plunged into doing whatever needed to be done here, for however long that might have been.

We have been able to put other people in place to help, and Mom can now go back to her own life. I will always be grateful that she was here for us.

When I was in college, I went to summer school one year at the University of Portland. I had always loved Oregon and wanted to find a way to visit, so I planned to take a class there and tour around. After just a few days, I realized what a mistake it was. It was a commuter school, everyone in my classes was in their thirties, and I was miserable. I called home and told Mom, and she suggested that instead of my coming home, she would come out and we would tour around together. She flew to Portland, I left my summer class, and we spent two weeks on the road together, traveling around the Oregon coast and up to Seattle. It was a gorgeous trip; the country there is amazingly beautiful! We had a lot of fun together, and related to each other as adults for the first time.

The key is, she dropped everything and came, just as she did when I had to go on bed rest during my pregnancy with Derek and Evan, just as she did the moment she heard that my brain MRI held bad news.

I am so grateful to know that I can always count on you, Mom and Dad. Thank you...I love you.

February 15

Just Say Yes

For many people, their first inclination when asked is to say no. This most often comes up in parenting—when children ask for something, our natural reaction is to say no. How much different if we say yes! People feel the need to control their children, their actions, their reactions...why not honor exactly who they are and let them be their own guides? Why do we feel that our perspective or opinion is better or more valuable because we are bigger or have lived longer?

I have consciously and actively given my kids as much freedom as possible to choose their own paths. If that means indulging in an activity for hours on end, so be it. They are getting something out of it and would not continue to do it if they were not.

When Adam was very young, he would watch the task bar fill as he downloaded Napster music (before the lawsuits). He was probably figuring out some kind of rates in his head as he watched...who knows? If he was not getting something out of it, he would not have been doing it. Because he had the freedom then to choose his own path and how to use his own time, he continues to do so now. Last week, he began an AP Economics course through Florida Virtual School. He completed his first module in two days, working many hours each day as he immersed himself in the subject. When my kids are interested in something, they plunge in wholeheartedly!

While this perspective may not work in all households, it works in mine. Derek and Evan discovered *Futurama*, a fun, irreverent show that Adam had shared with me. They watched the end of an episode that Adam was showing me, and loved it! They created their own Futurama Marathon, watching for two days straight until they had watched every episode. I am not suggesting this works for everyone, just that it was exactly what worked for them. They were clearly getting something out of the experience or they would not have continued. Within a few days, they were saturated.

The idea to just say yes and not try to control everything applies to simpler, smaller things like what they choose to eat or what activity they choose to do. This is the unschooling philosophy at work, but it is truly all of life. If they would like to eat lunch at 2 p.m. instead of 1 p.m. because they are in the middle of a project, that is perfectly fine with me. I do not need to choose for them. They choose for themselves.

You have to trust that they will eventually come to discover what they love. A friend's daughter recently started to write, after years of saying she did not want to write. She is now working on a novel for hours each day.

So much of the philosophy is about not needing to control anyone else. Because of course the reality is that you cannot control others, only yourself. So why not start teaching that idea when they are kids? Control is an illusion that often puts people in a very negative place because as they realize they cannot control others or situations, they get frustrated and try to clamp down and control even more

Every day, I realize more and more that there is no need to try to control anything. If you take each day and each moment as it comes, it is so freeing. It empties your mind and declutters your brain. You don't need to have an opinion or a way to do something better or even a plan for how things "should" be done. If you just allow life to unfold before you, how much more pleasant and enjoyable it will become!

This is not to say that you can never have a goal or an idea of how you want to make things better in your own life. It is simply that you have that idea, and you allow yourself to get there moment by moment. If you are not fully present in the moment, your goal will be more elusive. In *A New Earth*, Eckhart Tolle talks about looking up a phone number in the phone book. While your ultimate goal may be to find that number, your step-by-step process is finding the phone book, looking up the number and dialing it. Each step along the way can be fully embraced as being in the moment. From a larger perspective, if you have in mind something you'd like to change in your life, take it step-by-step, and embrace each moment along the way, rather than thinking that happiness can only be attained once your goal has been reached. You will never reach that elusive happiness if you can only find it once your task is complete, as each step, each moment, brings happiness and completeness.

Just say yes to each moment, to your kids, to your loved ones, to yourself.

February 17

Medical Update

I am feeling so good right now! I just got back from my trainer/physical therapist/mental guru and not only did he help my legs and arms function again, but we had an amazing discussion, as we always do. It is incredible when like minds connect. He is a natural healer, for the mind, body and spirit. It is hard to find people who are so positive and in a similar place as I am, so I find it invigorating to be with him. We both enjoy helping and bringing insights into others' lives, and are grateful for the opportunity to do so.

The steroids have really been taking a toll on me; I felt like my legs and arms were so heavy that it was difficult to lift them. I could walk, but the stairs were difficult, and even lifting my legs into a car was hard. Now, I feel like I am almost running! Not really, but soon!

The doctors told me today I can start weaning off the steroids; this is wonderful news! The side effects from the chemo and radiation have, thankfully, been minimal. However, the steroids I have been on, which help to protect my brain from swelling during the radiation treatment, have affected every part of my body. I can't wait to be off of them.

Now, I have only four more brain treatments! About a

week after the radiation is complete, I will get another MRI of my brain. Hopefully, most of the lesions will have disappeared due to the treatment. Whatever is left, they will stereotactically remove (highly focused radiation, specifically to any remaining lesions). Then, I will have a totally clear brain! LOL!

Two weeks ago, I had a CT of my chest, and the tumor there is gone. Gone! Chemo and radiation are truly medical miracles.

After they are done with any clean-up of my brain, the doctors will continue to follow me every month or so. I will have another PET scan in about three months and we will go from there.

When I asked the doctor what to do in the meantime, his answer was, "Live. Just live your life."

February 24

And Sometimes, the Answer Is No

Last time, I spoke about saying yes and keeping options open. Sometimes, you also have to know yourself and your kids and know when to just say no. Volumes have been written about how to help busy people say no to overcommitting themselves.

I have never been one to sign up for lots of activities, for myself or my kids. Adam taught me early on—when he was less than a year old—that he needed time at home and did not like to be out every day. He was just a happier child when he had plenty of down time at home. And sleep was always paramount to me, with all the kids. When Adam went to preschool, I was fortunate to have a babysitter for Jaron so that he could nap. And when Jaron was in school, the same babysitter came so that Derek and Evan could nap. I was able to keep the babies home and not have to drag them around; their nap schedules were not disturbed.

Once Adam was old enough to stay home by himself, and then when he was old enough to watch the other kids, it was such a pleasure. He no longer complained about going to the grocery store because he could stay home and do his own thing.

We never did a lot of lessons, only tried one sport, drifted in and out of co-ops, some years more than others. In terms of lessons, this was what I learned: if they ask for it, give it to them. If not, don't. (My wise neighbor whose kids are a few years older than mine told me this years ago.) With Jaron, I had searched for Irish Step dancing lessons for him for two years, when he was four and five years old. I found private lessons when he was five, and the lessons killed the dancing for him. He had asked when he was four, but by the time I found someone, he just wanted to teach himself. He did not want someone else telling him the steps. The same thing happened with his art: he took lessons for a few years, but then he wanted to teach himself and stopped taking lessons.

In regard to bridge, we helped Adam find teachers when he was seven years old. By the time he was ten, he found his own mentors and teachers and he now seeks counsel from the best players in the world.

In his wonderful book, *Last Child in the Woods*, Richard Louv speaks of the opportunity to just let our kids play. Kids are over-scheduled for many reasons, he says, but one is the false fear that just letting them play outside—building tents, playing kickball with the neighbors—will deprive children of opportunities if they are not constantly learning something. But they are constantly learning, from everything, especially things that don't look like lessons.

Something Extraordinary

For some families, a whirlwind of lessons and sports and late evenings works. For us, being home quietly with just a few activities out each week works. A park day, a workshop every few weeks, and a Pokemon League each week allow my kids the chance to just be.

And right now, I need that same chance. Because I am completely able to listen to what my body needs and rest when I need to, I have done exactly that. I even cancelled lunch yesterday with friends I had not seen for a while because I was just too tired and needed to rest.

My brother in Indianapolis offered me a very unique opportunity in May. He is running a half-marathon there, and we thought it would be a neat experience for him to push me in wheelchair and run with me. It sounded like such a great idea, but I have absolutely no idea how I will feel in May. The doctor said it may be months before I get my strength back. So I decided it was better not to overcommit, but to take each day as it comes.

So that is my plan, as it has been all along: to take each day as it comes, to say yes to opportunities, and no to too many commitments.

Slow down your family life if you find yourself out every evening. Say no to activities that aren't meaningful to you. Pare down your commitments. Just be...

March 3

Medical Update

I had my follow-up brain MRI today. As expected, there are a handful of lesions that, thus far, have not been resolved by the chemo and radiation. One of the main areas with lesions is in my cerebellum, which controls balance, my only neurological problem all along.

I will meet with my doctor again next week to discuss the exact plan of action: whether to address certain lesions stereotactically (very specifically) or with IMRT (a little broader). This week, he will meet with the physicist to come up with a game plan. I feel so distinguished!

Since I finished treatment last week, I have really enjoyed not having to be up and out the door each morning. And I am very grateful to not have to be, as I am completely exhausted!

I have thankfully been sleeping through the night, almost every night, waking up around 7:30 or 8:00 a.m., and am back asleep by 10:30 or 11:00 each morning. I nap for several hours before lunch.

When my dear friends came to visit this past weekend, I stayed up with them later than I normally would have. I just slept it off the next day.

I am weaning off the steroids, and the brain radiation is

catching up to my body, so I just need to sleep it all off. The nurse today used pregnancy as an analogy. She said it takes nine months to get through that, and many more months for your body to get back to any kind of normality. I have been in treatment for three months, so I cannot expect to feel normal for a while yet.

And I am totally fine with that! I have no expectations. Every day is a new adventure.

I am very thankful to be weaning off the steroids, as every day the puffiness goes down just a bit. The amazing thing is that since everybody reacts differently, there is no way to know how long it will take or what it will feel like as I wean off. I am down to two milligrams (mg) from eight mg of dexamethasone, which is a huge drop, but still not enough for my body to start functioning on its own yet. That will not happen until my dose is down to .75 mg. I have no idea when this will be.

Again, I am fine with that. Whatever the doctors feel I need, I will continue to take. Perhaps after this next round of brain radiation, they may be able to drop me to a level of steroids where my body (adrenals specifically) can again function on its own. If not, whenever it will be, will be.

My mom heads back to Maryland on Saturday. Thank you, Mom, again, for all you have done for all of us these past few months. We could never have done it without you!

Cathy, our nanny from when the kids were younger, will be starting back with us on Monday, so it will be a new adventure for us all.

My dad will stay for another month to continue to help with the kids and driving, and just being grandpa.

And I continue to take each day as the gift that it is.

March 8

Heighten Your Senses

March is my favorite month. Not just because it is my birthday month, but because it is the beginning of spring, when nature heightens our senses and makes it much easier to concentrate on the now.

The wind and gentle warm breezes are my favorite things, and in March, they are out in full force. The breeze caressing your skin is the most delicious feeling.

I have been reading Jean Houston's book *A Passion for the Possible*. In it, she writes of how to sharpen your senses. So many people go through life without paying much attention to sensory input. However, children are highly attuned to it. Autistic people are hyper-attuned to it, due to their inability to tune out extraneous sensory input. I suggest there is a happy medium, that we can increase our awareness way beyond what our normal is, and enjoy life a great deal more, as well as help ourselves focus on the now.

Think of someone you know who truly enjoys food, or surrounds herself with flowers or candles, or feels a rapture when listening to a great symphony. Is that person living a richer life? I think so.

Smell

When I had my sinus surgery ten years ago, I lost my sense of smell for about six months. I was incredibly sad to think I would never smell certain smells again. It did come back, and some smells were not so pleasant, but I was happy to have them all.

Last fall, I made it a point to drive to my apartment with the windows down. I had always driven with the windows up, in my own sanitary car with sanitary air conditioning, because I was afraid of the pollen. But I purposely wanted to experience things differently, experience more of life. Driving down the street, I was amazed at the smells at each point along the way, such as the scent of each restaurant's food, houses that had fires in the fireplace, a tire store; smells that I had forgotten existed because I had kept myself away from them.

Suggestions in Houston's book include sniffing spices, surrounding yourself with flowers and candles, noting the shampoo, soap and toothpaste smells you encounter each day.

Smell is the most evocative sense. If we smell something from our childhood, we will be transported back to that time, along with all the accompanying memories and emotions. I remember an episode of M*A*S*H in which Hawkeye found himself in a marsh in Korea and relived a childhood trauma based solely on the smell. Rather than relive a trauma as he did, if you are able, find someplace that brings you back to a happy time from long ago. Go there and sniff…

Taste

While taste is closely related to smell, it is unique. At the moment, I cannot taste much of anything, as the chemo has dulled my taste buds. Most things taste the same to me, with a few exceptions, such as red pear, Fuji apples, cherry tomatoes (is there a "red" taste?). I hope my taste will come back at some point, just as my smell came back after my sinus surgery. In the meantime, I am eating what I need, regardless of taste. Jaron once commented that the obesity epidemic would be cured quickly if we had no taste buds. I do believe he is right, as I make choices based on what the healthiest foods are, rather than what tastes good, which generally is fatty and full of sugar!

But everyone can make subtle changes in what one eats. Even if you eat the same foods, you can slow down and enjoy your food more.

Suggestions from Houston include visiting ethnic restaurants and trying new flavors, going to a specialty deli and trying a new cheese or wine, baking bread, and trying exotic fruits. Anytime you introduce your taste buds to something new, you enliven them.

I did not eat meals in my apartment, but I did have late-night desserts! One night, I stopped at McDonald's and got apple pie. I had not eaten that since high school, yet I remembered the taste, smell, feel on my tongue, and the circumstance of hanging out with my high school friends after the football games. Because taste is closely related to smell, it can be similarly evocative.

I was so excited when I found Quisp cereal last year! I could not wait to taste it again, as it had been off the market since I was about ten years old. But when I tasted it, it was sickeningly sweet and tasted like cardboard. I had a similar disappointment when I bought Pop-Tarts last week. I had not tasted them in years, and found them cloyingly sweet, a disappointing memory.

If anyone ever finds Fudgetown cookies by Burry, I would love to try them and see if they still taste the same! With cookies, there is the whole sensory experience: with Fudgetown cookies, we popped out the button of chocolate in the middle. Some people lick the creme filling of an Oreo, while others dunk the whole thing. There is so much more to eating than just the food!

When my girlfriends from my early teen years recently visited me, we recalled all the different pizza places in which we had hung out. We could still taste each different kind of pizza. As all the restaurants have since closed, they are but memories.

I would love to hear others' memories of favorite childhood foods, and the memories they evoke. Please do share!

Hearing

When the kids were young, we always used to have music on in the background. It was soothing orchestral music, always very calming. After smell and taste, hearing is the next most evocative sense. Sounds go directly to a part of our brain that controls our emotions, which is the theory behind sound therapies. When you hear a particular song from your teen years, you may picture the whole scene and feel all the emotions you felt then.

Jaron and I were in a restaurant once where the songs were all from the '80s. Of course, I knew them all; some from high school, some from college. As each song came on, I told him a memory of that song and that time, and sang along. He was amazed, and embarrassed.

Some people listen to music all the time. Adam is never without. I do not know the research into the teen brain, but I imagine there is some reason for it. However, in his case, he has listened since he was four or five years old. Always classic rock. For him, that part of his brain needs to be engaged so that he can focus on other things. Otherwise, his mind wanders.

I have taken to silence. While I listen to some mix CDs that kind friends have sent, I am mostly content with silence.

A friend told me how she enjoys sitting outside and just listening to the birds. This is something else March has brought. The parrots at the beach are back. The birdsongs really do calm you.

Some suggestions from Houston include reading poetry aloud, listening to different types of music than you normally do, singing, and going to a park and just listening.

Touch

This is probably one of the most neglected and elusive senses. And yet, it is what connects us as humans. Both touching and being touched are essential. Though the skin is your largest organ, the touch receptors vary over the different parts of your skin, in terms of pain, temperature, pressure and touch. Your fingertips are most sensitive; the middle of your back, the least.

When Adam was three years old, we used to dance in the rain. I never use umbrellas; I would much rather feel the rain on my skin. When the hurricanes came one year, Adam, Jaron and I went outside to feel the wind on our bodies. Evan has always wanted to be in constant contact with me. When we would go to a show, as long as I kept my hand on him, he was fine. Now, he asks for massage all the time. When Derek was two years old, I would hold him and pat his back. He, in turn, would pat my back. I used to say that I wish I had a touch camera so that I would always remember the feel of his hand on my shoulder. And just by stating that, I do feel it.

I used to go for massage regularly, but have felt odd doing so since I have been in treatment. Some therapists feel it is healing; others are reluctant to potentially spread anything through the lymphatic system. When I went to my trainer a few weeks ago, he did massage parts of my back and legs that had not been touched in months. I had no idea how sore and tender the muscles were! While I am weaning off the steroids right now, my muscles are incredibly achy, but I patiently wait, knowing it will all resolve shortly.

Suggestions from Jean Houston for heightening the sense of touch include visiting a fabric store, touching different types of plants and flowers, getting (and giving) a massage, hugging others, and using different strokes on your own skin to learn what brings you pleasure.

Proprioception

This is the sense of where your body is in space—an area in which an occupational therapist (OT) specializes. Derek and Adam both went through OT for various proprioceptive issues, and it helped tremendously. For me, this is an interesting one at the moment, because I do not feel like my body is my own. Due to the steroids, I do not feel like myself or look like myself at all. It is indeed an odd feeling, and as I lie in bed sometimes, I feel very detached from my body.

Mindfulness, meditation and breathwork help put us back in our bodies. I have spoken before about how one knows something fully and completely in one's body: "shackles on/shackles off." I still have that sense, but do look forward to having my body feel like my own again at some point!

Vision

Vision is our most used sense: 70 percent of our sensory receptors are in our eyes. When Adam went through vision therapy to improve how his eyes worked in conjunction with each other, it improved not only his vision, but his balance, his ability to follow directions, and his understanding of the world around him. Vision informs everything we do.

Color is a large part of our enjoyment. The walls and carpet of my house are off-white and the cabinets bleached pine. We have black granite and black tables. There is no color; it is all neutral. It is beautiful, but I have recently felt the need for bold color. My friend Wendy came to visit me and gave me a very thoughtful gift that only a close friend could give. She, along with other dear friends Ellen and Betty, painted my room. I chose the colors and bought the paint before Wendy came, and the three of them spent the weekend painting. It was one of the most generous gifts I have ever received. Now, as I revel in my forest-green and seafoam-green walls, I think of the kindness they bestowed and the joy that color has brought into my life.

Something Extraordinary

Jaron is an artist; he naturally sees details and depth that I do not. Evan too sees small details which to me are insignificant, but which pop out at him. When he was two years old, Evan would point out to me some detail in a book that was drawn slightly differently than it had been sixty pages earlier. Now, his favorite games to play on the computer are Hidden Object games. We can develop this ability to notice small details if we choose.

How to see more intently? Visit an art gallery and look at paintings you would not normally view. Look at a flower and describe every detail; once you have described as much as you think you can, look further, and describe even more detail. Do this mentally; imagine a place or an item and fully describe it, in words or images, in your mind. Sight is probably the sense that our mind engages in most fully, and is easiest for us to recreate. We can visualize much more easily than we can engage any other sense.

Guided imagery has been used to help heal. While visualizing a scene is a large part of this, the more senses you are able to activate, the more successful the healing. The whole brain can work to heal.

Regardless of your purpose in heightening your senses, nature can play a large part in helping. March reminds us of the role nature plays. For those up north, a spring thaw, and for us in Florida, gentle birdsongs and warm breezes. (November here is akin to March up north, when the stifling heat breaks and the coolness arrives.)

Some are more touched by the water, some by the woods. I prefer to lie on a forest floor and be surrounded by the smell of pine, the sun streaming through the treetops, the screech of a far-off hawk, the cool soft touch of the pine needles.

In *A Year By the Sea*, Joan Anderson says you cannot be neurotic in nature. Step out, enjoy a walk, surround yourself with the smells, sounds, touch and sights of March. It is a beautiful month.

March 11

So What Now?

I met with both the radiation and medical oncologists, and for the first time, I have had to make a decision about my treatment. Up until this point, all has been pretty much laid out. There was a question early on regarding whether they would radiate my lung or brain first, and both doctors agreed on the more aggressive treatment of lung first (although the Moffitt Cancer Center doctor disagreed).

Now, the radiation oncologist has recommended further treatment of my brain right now, whereas the medical oncologist has recommended waiting a few weeks and seeing what a follow-up MRI shows. The lesions on the MRI could be scar tissue or they could be cancer; they just don't know. And the only way to know is to wait and see if they grow, shrink, or stay the same. If the lesions were elsewhere in the body, they could biopsy them. But in the brain, you wait or you guess.

You can only tolerate a certain amount of radiation to your brain over your lifetime, so I have chosen to wait a few weeks and see what the next MRI will show. The radiation oncologist accepts this choice, though it is not his first recommendation. It just seems to make sense to me to keep more options open. If there are any changes in the meantime, we will reevaluate, but a few weeks seems a very short and reasonable time to wait to ensure that what they are treating indeed needs to be treated.

It does give me a sense of what others who have lots of medical options must go through. I do not envy their choices. While it may be that some want lots of options because it gives them a sense of control, I have enjoyed not having to choose.

I have all kinds of scans scheduled at the end of the month: CT, MRI and PET. So we will see what they show and go from there.

I also have an appointment at Moffitt Cancer Center on April 7 to join the clinical trial I mentioned earlier. At that time, they will randomize my case and place me in the study. So I ask everyone to hope for me to be placed exactly where I am supposed to be, in the control group or experimental group.

A wise woman once told me that one should not ask the Universe for something specific, as that limits the options and you just never know what is best. She suggested asking for the highest and greatest good for all. So I will ask for things to be exactly as they are meant to be.

I am down to one milligram of steroid daily. That is what I most look forward to being done with!

And when I get my taste back, I will have to try a HoHo - Lil' Debbie taste test.

March 15

Rhythms

This subject was prompted by a conversation with Derek. He was in my room the other morning, and the bright room suddenly got dark. He looked up at the lights and saw that they were still off and had not changed. He was confused until he realized that the sun had gone behind the clouds, and made the room very dark very quickly. He did not immediately know what had caused the darkness because in the rooms he spends more of his time in, this phenomenon did not occur. In the living room, there are enough windows and enough light that, while there may be a slight decrease in light, there is enough that it is not dramatic. In the computer room, the light is always on, or Derek is facing the screen, so he does not see the change in light. In his bedroom, the shutters are always down, so it is always dark in there, no matter what the time of day. If he wants light in his room, he turns on the light overhead. There is no natural rhythm to the light of his day. It is all artificial (except for the living room area, which reflects the reality of outside).

It is the same as the artificial environment we create in our cars when we keep the windows closed and do not experience the smells of the world. It reminds me of the science fiction movies in which the society lives in a dome: all is artificially created and controlled.

There are ways to maintain natural rhythms, both daily and throughout the year.

This post was also prompted by Daylight Savings Time, which began this past weekend. I am not a fan of Daylight Savings Time. I prefer Standard Time. I have loved waking up to the increase in sunlight as it floods my room. I can tell exactly what time it is by the amount of light, and have been waking up just about the time the sunlight fully arrives, around 7:30 a.m. Now, it is still dark at 7:30 a.m., and though I may adjust as the months progress, it is just not natural for it to still be light in Florida after 9:00 p.m., as it will be in the summertime.

Saskatchewan has recently voted to remain on standard time all year long. Until 2005, parts of Indiana did not observe Daylight Savings Time. Arizona and Hawaii still do not. They maintain Standard Time all year long.

When Adam was younger, he had great difficulty changing from Standard to Daylight Savings Time. He was very exacting with his sleep, and it took months for him to change times. Now, as a teenager, he stays up half the night, so time changes mean nothing to him. And the other kids have always done remarkably well when we have traveled. Even when we went to Hawaii, they adjusted beautifully. Still, I would prefer that we have one time and stick to it, rather than changing mid-year.

Sleep has always been a huge issue for me. When Adam was born, my friend Lynn gave me *Healthy Sleep Habits, Happy Child* by Marc Weissbluth. One of the aphorisms in it that I always lived by was "Never wake a sleeping child." I had a babysitter for Jaron when I needed to pick Adam up from preschool because naptime was sacred.

As they grew, I embraced a new aphorism, one I learned from Stephanie Tolan, a leader and elder of the gifted community. I talked with her when Jaron was in school, concerned that he should be homeschooled as well. Her advice was, "Never move a happy child."

This advice is a logical extension of the sleep philosophy from when they were younger. Now, it speaks to the idea that you don't mess with them when they are in the middle of something. This goes for anyone. A different way may not be a better way, and there is no reason to change something just because you can. Let others figure it out for themselves. I see this tendency all the time: to interrupt people, especially kids, because someone thinks they know a better way.

There is a process termed "flow," coined by positive psychology researcher Mihály Csíkszentmihályi, in which a person gets so engrossed in whatever he or she is doing that he or she loses all track of time. There is spontaneous joy as a person is completely immersed with intense focus. This is when a person is truly engaged in life. One should never interrupt a person when he has "flow"! Think back to an activity that was so joyful for you that you just wanted to continue it for hours on end. See if there is any way to bring that into your life, and see how naturally the rhythm of the day can flow.

Regarding a different kind of rhythm, I have a theory about times and parts of the country that I think would make a great Ph.D. thesis for someone. I believe that one of the reasons people in the Midwest are, in general, kinder and more temperate than those people on the East or West Coast is because of prime time TV. The people on the coasts generally stay up until at least 11 p.m. because that is when prime time is over. The people in the central and mountain time zones (Midwest), are generally in bed by 10 p.m.

I think this affects how kids grow up in the different parts of the country, and affects their manner and how they view the world. When you are growing up, you think everyone has a similar experience as you. But when I got to college and met someone who grew up in Chicago, and found out that she went to bed at 10, it started me thinking. Now that I live in Florida, I realize that most textbooks show snow in the winter and do not apply to Florida schoolchildren, or to those in most of the Southwest. But I grew up in Maryland, where everything seemed "normal." I guess everything seems normal wherever you are, until you live somewhere else and realize that yours is only a small view of the world.

Yearly rhythms are accounted for by the Jewish calendar. There is a holiday in every month except one. My family is not observant, so we do not celebrate most of the holidays, but they are there, and I can understand the reasons for having a special day each month. Modern society has recreated this idea, but with greeting card holidays instead. I do not personally celebrate any of them—I think they are nonsense. My kids would rather celebrate National Donut Day than Valentine's Day!

Sometimes, years just roll along and we do not even realize that another one has passed. But some years are more memorable than others, and we think to ourselves, "Last year at this time..." I believe that is how each succeeding year will be for me now. I know 2011 will, as 2010 brought so many changes in my life. And now, I am much more attuned to each day, and think about what happened last year at each day, while thoroughly being here, now.

March 21

Hold Lightly

My friend Ellen shared a delightful story: she was having lunch with a new friend whom she had met through Toastmasters, an organization she had recently joined. She admired the woman's fleece sweatshirt and explained that it sported her favorite colors, and that she loved fleece. The woman took off the jacket and gave it to her. Ellen started to protest and insist that she not take it, but decided to resist the urge, because it would make the woman happy to give her new friend something she would enjoy, and it would make Ellen happy to have the shirt and think of her new friend whenever she wore it.

They both illustrated beautifully the principle of not holding objects (or people) too tightly. In *Saying Yes to Change*, Gordon Dveirin explains, "The open hand that lets go with ease receives just as easily." It is graceful to let others help you, or give things to you. And it is a joy to give! My friend Lynn's young son loves science and math. It has been great fun scouring my house to find books and puzzles that he will enjoy; Lynn was kind enough to share pictures of the happiness on his face as he reads and plays with them.

There is a reason we all feel good when we declutter, clean out and lighten up. Stuff is just stuff, and it serves a purpose for a time, but then, it is time to get rid of it and clear out. How much lighter we feel when we are not burdened by stuff everywhere. I have mentioned before that in my apartment, I only had a couch, a bed and a computer. Everywhere else was empty, and it was a joy to not have stuff.

It can be hard to let go because we may feel an emotional attachment. But with technology, that is easy to take care of: take a picture or a video, and then get rid of the object.

People often hold onto relationships way beyond the time that they are productive also. A friend sent me this poem:

> *People come into your life for a reason, a season, or a lifetime.*
> *When you know which one it is, you will know what to do for that person.*
>
> *When someone is in your life for a reason, it is usually to meet a need you have expressed.*
> *They have come to assist you with a difficulty, to provide you with guidance and support, to aid you physically, emotionally or spiritually.*
> *They are there for the reason you need them to be.*
> *Then, without any wrongdoing on your part, or at an inconvenient time, this person will say or do something to bring the relationship to an end.*
> *Sometimes they die. Sometimes they walk away. Sometimes they act up and force you to take a stand.*
> *What we must realize is that our need has been met, our desire fulfilled, their work is done and now it is time to move on.*

Some people come into your life for a season, because your turn has come to share, grow, or learn.
They bring you an experience of peace, or make you laugh.
They may teach you something you have never done.
They usually give you an unbelievable amount of joy.
Believe it, it is real. But only for a season.

Lifetime relationships teach you lifetime lessons, things you must build upon in order to have a solid emotional foundation. Your job is to accept the lesson, love the person and put what you have learned to use in all other relationships and areas of your life.

When I was younger, I used to believe the poem:

If you love something, set it free.
If it comes back, it is yours forever,
If it doesn't, it never was.

I no longer believe this to be the case. I believe that relationships exist for a reason, a season, or a lifetime. Just because something doesn't come back does not mean it was never yours. It just means that your time together is over and it is time to move on. This is true of relationships, objects, anything. Just because something is over does not mean that it was not real, important and special while it lasted. The time has just passed.

Think back to when your children were growing up. At each successive difficulty, you probably uttered something like, "This is just a phase." And if you were wise, you said it with each joy also. In *Coming to Our Senses*, Jon Kabat-Zinn reminds us that the most useful phrase one can utter is, "This too shall pass." It reminds us that everything is fleeting, both the joys and the sorrows. While this may sound depressing, it is another reminder to celebrate the now because the now is always changing.

People are afraid of change and sometimes cling stubbornly to the way things are. This is called the Chinese finger-trap or pickle-jar mentality. The finger-trap is when you place a finger in each end of the woven cylinder of straw. The harder you try to pull your fingers out, the tighter the trap closes around your finger. For the pickle jar, you plunge your hand in the jar to pull out the pickle, but cannot extract your hand because it is gripping the pickle. The only way to get out of either trap is to let go. As soon as you relax and stop struggling, you are free.

Lately, any time I have found myself tensing up or getting upset in any way, I hear the mantra I shared earlier, "Let it go, let it go, let it go," and I instantly relax.

While we know that our children are with us for a fixed amount of time, we rarely think of other relationships in a time-defined way. But if we think of them as a reason, a season, or a lifetime, we will not be as disappointed when some people are no longer in our lives.

While I have recently had the pleasure of reconnecting with friends from 20, 25 and 30 years ago, and it has been amazing, I also have friends that I have not reconnected with, because we served each other a purpose at the time, and that purpose has passed. There is no one at fault, and it is not a relationship that needs to be repaired; its time has simply passed. It can be a positive memory.

This comes back around to having no regrets. I have had many friends over the years with whom I am no longer in touch. Some people may feel badly about those relationships, or feel there was something they could have done to maintain those friendships. I accept that they were the right relationships at the right time. I am not saying you should change friends like you change hats, but that if a relationship no longer serves either of you, and is a strain rather than a joy, than perhaps it is time to move on, with no regrets. If you recognize that there is nothing wrong with this, that "this too, passed," then you can move on without burning bridges. There may be some friends with whom you are able to reconnect, and discover that what brought you together in the first place still exists. What a pleasure!

The other problem I have with the poem, "If You Love Something, Set It Free" is the idea that anyone "belongs" to anyone. We all belong only to ourselves. It is only when we realize this that we find who we truly are and what our purpose truly is.

I refer again to the Buddhist monks, who have few earthly attachments, either to things or people. The second Noble Truth in Buddhism is, "The origin of suffering is attachment." This refers to objects, ideas and people. The idea is not to cling to anything too tightly. You can recognize this Zen-state in one who does not let things bother him. There is a calm and peacefulness surrounding him.

I rarely react to much anymore. I think sometimes it drives those around me crazy! But it is just much more comfortable and easy...when you hold all lightly.

March 28

Celebrate!

I had the good fortune yesterday of celebrating my birthday with those who have supported me these past few months through rides, food, and taking care of the kids. I wanted to say thank you to everyone, and there seemed no better time than my birthday to do so.

A friend pointed out that after about age nine or ten, we do not usually have birthday parties with our friends. Perhaps a Sweet 16 or a special celebration to signify turning 21, but not a party with our own friends. And even milestone ages are often not celebrated because people are hung up on getting older and not wanting others to know how old they are. Come on...if each day is a gift, how much more so is each year?

I enjoyed a wonderful day of celebration with my friends and their families. As homeschoolers, we have always invited the whole family to our parties. Each child invites his friends, but siblings are always included, as are parents. We have never had a drop-off party, as that is just not how we do things. But this time, it was not just the parents of the kids' friends (although they were there too, because they are my friends), but *my* friends too.

This led to some wonderful nostalgia as several of us who have known each other for over fifteen years recalled how we first met and talked about some of our interactions from the early days. These friends from long ago have reached out and supported me with rides and food and a listening ear.

As I have mentioned before, being around other people energizes me. I was pleasantly surprised to see that I was able to visit with everyone the whole afternoon. People came in two shifts, so it was never too crowded, yet there was always someone to visit with. And I was able to sit as people came to me to talk. Friends from different parts of my life met, and as always, new connections were made, which I love helping to facilitate. The kids, too, renewed old ties, and played dodge ball until they were dripping with sweat. They connected with friends old and new.

I was especially touched that one of the guests, who shares my birthday (same day and year), chose to celebrate with me. Two other guests have daughters whose birthdays are on the same day as well, yet they were there to celebrate with us.

I was overwhelmed only once during the day, when everyone gathered to sing "Happy Birthday" as I blew out the candle on my cake. As I looked around at everyone who was there to celebrate with me, I was overcome with gratitude for the good fortune with which I am blessed. I was so touched that these people were there for me, and had been there for me, and will continue to be there for me. I am grateful too for those who were not able to physically be there with me, but have been there with your words, your support, and your love. I thank you all.

April 4

Secrets of a Life Well Lived

I went to the woods because I wished to live deliberately, to front only the essential facts of life, and see if I could not learn what it had to teach, and not, when I came to die, discover that I had not lived.

– Henry David Thoreau

I dedicate this entry to my grandfather, Zadye. Today is his birthday; he would have been 105. He lived to the age of 96, was able to hold four of his great-grandsons for their bris (boy's traditional Jewish circumcision at eight days old), and inspired his eight grandchildren with his never-wavering love, support and admiration. He was my wise elder.

I promised earlier that I would get back to a book that I mentioned which impacted me greatly, *The Five Secrets You Must Learn Before You Die* by John Izzo.

Izzo interviewed hundreds of wise elders, people who had been recommended to him as those "who had found happiness and wisdom," to discover what they had learned about life. He asked questions and listened to their stories. He found that five common themes emerged as these elders reminisced about their lives.

1. Be True to Yourself

Don't try to be someone you are not. Deep down, we all know who we truly are: that part of us that is our essential self, when no one else is looking, when we are in conversation only with ourselves. For those who live with integrity, this true self is reflected in the same persona in most situations. Don't give up your core values in an attempt to benefit the situation.

2. Leave No Regrets

Izzo found that people did not regret trying new things, taking a chance or any other endeavor they had been unsure about, even if they failed. What people did regret was what they had not done. From asking someone to dance to starting your own business to buying a home that is a financial stretch but in the long run could pay off well, the people who were most contented ventured beyond their comfort zone rather than staying safe in a corner.

3. Become Love

Without a doubt, the common thread of all religions, all self-help advice, all philosophies, is love. Looking back on their lives, the elders said that in the end, the relationships they had were all that really mattered. This is not news. This is something we all know. However, those who live well ensure that this is a priority. They choose relationship over winning an argument, over money, over all else.

4. Live the Moment

Rather than living in the past or fearing for the future, those who are content in life live in the present. I elaborate on this elsewhere, particularly in *Heighten Your Senses* (March 8). Izzo met people who, through various means, were able to be fully present. Their comfort and joy were clear.

5. Give More Than You Take

To be content, one should not think only of oneself, but of others as well. If you are feeling badly about yourself or your situation, the surest way to feel better is to help others. I have written about ways to help your community in *Leave the World Better Than You Found It* (February 3). Leave a legacy of good.

Izzo's powerful book was made into a PBS television series and thus able to reach a larger audience. Its lessons, and the manner in which they were derived, touched me. They are a valuable recipe for a life well-lived.

April 7

Medical Update

I have been resting, reading and reviving. Thankfully, during treatment, I wasn't that tired. But since treatment's completion, I cannot imagine how I got up and went every day. I finished weaning off the steroids almost two weeks ago, and it has been a rough ride. I have completely lost my appetite, but have forced myself to eat and drink as much as I possibly can. I have lost ten pounds (but still weigh 15 more than when I first got sick), mostly water weight from the steroids. I am no longer puffy and swollen.

Last week, I had follow-up PET, CT and MRI scans. The PET showed no cancerous activity anywhere! The CT confirmed what the PET showed in my chest, and that is a lot of scar tissue and a partially collapsed lung. The doctor said this repairs itself eventually, but in the meantime, I need to take breaths as deep as possible to prevent pneumonia. Only having one good lung with which to breathe means that I get winded very easily and must sit most of the time.

The MRI of the brain showed no change in a few of the lesions and shrinkage in the others. Because there was no growth, the doctor agreed that we can again watch and wait.

I also went to Moffitt Cancer Center to find out about the clinical trial. I did meet the criterion for the study, but was randomly placed in the control group. This means that they will follow my case as someone to compare to those who get the vaccine that the study is investigating.

At first, I was very disappointed that I did not get placed in one of the experimental arms of the study. But as I wrote previously, I had hoped to be placed "exactly where I was supposed to be placed." I have to believe there was a reason I was not placed in the experimental arm—perhaps the side effects would have been too much for me? Perhaps I would have had some problem with the medication? Later in the day, after I found out, I received a card in the mail from a friend. The card read, "Keep Believing—What is Meant to Be Will Be—the things we want don't always come."

I discussed my disappointment with a wise friend who reminded me that it is fine to feel disappointed; just recognize it and acknowledge it, but do not judge it.

The hard part now is feeling like I am not doing anything. Before, I was doing treatment every day. Now it just feels like I am waiting. It is the doctors' job to monitor all the scans and any changes. It feels like they are just waiting to catch the cancer as soon as it comes back. But I do not want to let myself get caught up in that line of thought. I want to do exactly as my doctor had told me before, "Go live your life."

April 18

Seder

Tonight is the first night of Passover. This is the first year we are not having a Seder since Adam was two years old.

When he was three months old, we went to Maryland for my grandfather's 90th birthday party, and stayed for Seder. It was at my parents' house, and everyone was there for the first time in probably ten years. I felt like a kid again, except that I had my baby there with me!

When Adam was two, we changed to Daylight Saving Time the week before the Seder. He was a cranky mess, and I remember thinking that I really did not like Daylight Saving Time! That year, we had been going to Bagels & Blocks (a class for moms and toddlers at the temple). I would tell Adam that we were going to say "good morning" to God. I did not realize until Seder that he thought the preschool director must be God because we would say good morning to her each time we went to temple. At Seder, he asked if God was coming, and I said yes, God was everywhere. When he asked where her chair was, I realized whom he meant.

The years since then blend together so that I cannot say what year each Seder was, but I do know that over the years:

1. Our neighbors came with their five kids and we explained what a Seder was all about to this Christian family. They were fascinated and thought the food was delicious.

2. New homeschool friends who were Jewish but had never been to a Seder learned much more about their Jewish roots, and were grateful to us for teaching them about Passover.

3. Each of the kids in all the families that came were assigned a plague to demonstrate however they wished. We had a cow cookie jar with pox, flying frog tiddlywinks and a scientific explanation of why the first-born males likely were killed because they slept highest above the ground.

4. We built a tent under the spiral stairs several times, feeling we were in the desert, or at least a much more fun spot than the dining room!

5. Jaron learned the four questions in multiple languages and recited them with the appropriate accents.

6. When Derek and Evan were not quite one year old, my sister came to visit. She put them in their high chairs and pulled them up to the table. I had thought they were not yet ready, but they participated in the service just fine.

7. We have a picture of our toddlers on the couch, four or five families each with one or two kids, as we joked that these are the future Young Judea or USY officers photo.

8. Adam enjoyed sending the other kids on a scavenger hunt for the Afikomen. He would make riddles sending them around the house, one year hiding the Afikomen in a box of ice cream sandwiches.

Passover has always been my favorite holiday. I loved changing the dishes and using glass plates. My mom would always make my great-grandmother's sponge cake, and each year, see how high it could rise. I think 15 inches was the winner.

My parents would hold the first Seder at their house for my mom's side of the family, then we would go to my dad's sister's house for the second night for my dad's side, where there were always lots of people overflowing into every room. We got to taste wine. I got to see my cousins. And we got to stay up ridiculously late. We ate delicious Pechter's brownies (they were best when frozen!) and Seder mints. My job was polishing the silver: I can still smell and feel the silver polish (this was pre-Tarn-X).

I did not feel up to having a Seder this year. The rest of the family is going to the Seder at the temple, so they will still experience it. And my dad bought a box of Matza so we can have it here. Maybe next year...Next Year at Loni's House!

April 25

Neighbors

Our neighbors are moving. Not far. Only about 15 minutes away. But getting in a car is a whole different story than walking across the street.

They have been good neighbors. Over the years, we have borrowed from each other: tools, airbeds, a stick of butter, a dozen eggs. We held each other's keys. When we went on vacation, they collected our mail and newspapers, and when they went, we fed their cat, or gerbil, or whatever animal they had at the time. We went camping together once, and another time, just one of the kids came with us. The families fished together, both off the boats and off the docks.

We will miss being able to count on them in a pinch; when childcare fell through, we knew we could count on them to be a phone call away.

But there are two things which we will miss the most. First, Jaron and Bridgette have been best friends since her family first moved in seven years ago. He is having a really hard time knowing that she will no longer be a few steps away. Second, losing the kind of neighbors they were means the kids will end some of their innocent, carefree childhood.

Jaron and Bridgette have always gotten along famously.

They loved to bake, do projects, play games, try new things. Bridgette was almost always willing to go somewhere with us, and she always made the adventure more fun. Jaron could talk with her about anything. When I moved out, he went over to talk with Bridgette. When I got sick, he went over to talk with Bridgette.

Because he is homeschooled, Jaron does not have thirty kids he sees every day. His friendships are precious to him. And he is going to miss the casualness of wandering across the street for an afternoon of playing and then dinner, or having her call on a Saturday morning to see if she could come over as soon as she was done with her chores. His answer? I'll come over and help you finish them and then we can hang out together. Just a few weeks ago, Bridgette and her sister Jen came over to help get the house ready for my birthday party; they cleaned and cooked. Mom Cindy has been very supportive of me throughout the cancer process; she has searched for alternative therapies and clinical trials for me.

The other main reason we are so sad they are moving is that the relationship that we have enjoyed is so old-fashioned. In *Last Child in the Woods*, Robert Louv laments how our kids have lost their childhoods. No longer do they play at the end of the block, building castles in their imagination and playing some version of stickball. Well, with our neighbors, we did that. The kids would walk down to the beach and play in the tidepools and build sand castles. The parents projected a movie on the side of their house one spring evening, and served pizza and popcorn as we lay on blankets on the grass and watched. The kids trick-or-treated with dad Brian, and always had way more fun and got way more candy, than if they had gone without him. We played outdoor dodgeball in their backyard one spring night. The kids chased the ice cream man's truck together. We played tag in our front circle.

Kids' relationships with dads are so valuable because they are more unusual. Especially for my boys, they loved having another dad they could hang out with; even Adam, who is a tough sell, felt at home across the street. But it seems to be true for all kids. When I was in elementary school, it was such a special treat when my dad went on field trips with our class. Moms always went. When dads came, it was something special.

We did the kinds of things with them that families used to do with their neighbors. When I was a kid, there was a family like that in our neighborhood. My parents did not have a lot of friends, and I remember a sense of comfort watching my dad eat pretzels and drink beer with our neighbor. My siblings and I were friends with the kids, my parents were friends with the parents; it just seemed the way it should be. They moved away when I was seven or eight years old. Our parents stayed friends, and the dad signed my Ketubah, my marriage contract. But it was never the same after they moved away.

No longer could we just walk down the street to play. We saw them maybe once or twice a year for holidays. The easy simplicity of it all was gone, replaced by a formality that typified the rest of my friendships. I went to a private school, not a neighborhood school, so most of my friends lived far away. We had to have formal play dates and sleepovers. This typifies most kids' relationships today, which is why that of a neighborhood friend is so special, so cherished, so innocent and easy.

I am grateful my kids had a chance to know that kind of relationship, and sad that it is ending. My heart hurts the most for Jaron, but I think we are all losing something very special.

May 3

Sorry and Shame Are Four-letter Words

I have just about eliminated two phrases from my vocabulary: "I'm sorry…" and "It's a shame that…"

I'm not talking about the real kind of "I'm sorry," the kind when you have actually done something to cause some kind of emotional or physical harm to another person. I'm talking about the kind of "I'm sorry" that people utter almost as thoughtlessly as they do "I'm fine" when someone asks "How are you?"

If someone posts a message on Facebook that things are not going well, others often chime in with "I'm sorry," as if it is their fault or has anything at all to do with them. People do it with the best of intentions, expressing their sorrow that something has happened (or not happened). But what it really winds up doing is focusing on the negative.

I have a friend who has been very sick for several months. She was finally able to email me about what she has been going through. My first reaction, and what I typed back initially, was "I'm sorry you've had such a hard time." What does that focus on? The hard time. I deleted that sentence and replaced it with, "I'm glad you're feeling well enough now to email me." What does that focus on? The fact that she is better.

Something Extraordinary

Whenever you begin a sentence with this kind of "I'm sorry," it inevitably feels like a downer. No positives can come out of it, because it is inherently negative. Even when it feels appropriate, like at a funeral, see the difference in approach of "I'm sorry to hear of his passing," versus "I'm so glad I knew him." The former does express condolences, but stops the conversation, whereas the latter opens up positive interactions.

The other reason I have been trying to avoid the "I'm sorries" is that it makes me feel less burdened. Even if I am only saying the words, a part of me then takes on the responsibility for the other person's troubles. I need no more burdens than I already have! This is another way I have discovered to pare down what it is I worry about.

The phrase "It's a shame that..." often serves the same purpose. It is a negative phrase that I have been working hard to avoid. When my friend was sick and I decided not to say "I'm sorry you've been sick," I thought maybe I would say, "It's a shame you've been sick." It is less personal and does not put the burden on me, but on the general world. It makes it into an impersonal "it."

But it does not change the fact that it still puts a negative spin on whatever happened, or didn't happen. When it was a nice day out a while ago, I was told, "It's a shame the kids aren't outside playing." No, it's not a shame. It just is. It makes something neutral into a negative.

I have learned to accept so many things. Mostly just accepting that what is, is. It does not have to have a value judgment attached to it. It is only when we judge something that it brings an emotional reaction. Prior to judging, something just is. Actually, many things are if you just let them be. If you can suspend judgment, it saves a lot of emotional energy and helps you be more calm and steady. I do not react to things as much, and am much happier because of it.

If anyone catches me using either of these two phrases in my correspondence, please call me on it. I'm trying hard to eliminate them!

May 9

Retreat

I had the pleasure this past weekend of attending a Women's Retreat organized by my friend Ellen. We had spoken about this type of retreat back in October, when Ellen was involved in her yoga teacher's training classes, and I was reading *A Weekend to Change Your Life* by Joan Anderson. Ellen wanted to find ways to share yoga with more people, and we both longed for opportunities for connection with friends of friends, a way for women to come together and strengthen one another.

I contacted Ellen back in February, reminding her that we had thought that spring would be a perfect time, when the weather was not yet hot in Florida. She ran with it at that point, contacting the Franciscan Center in Tampa, where she had recently gone on a Silent Retreat. She arranged all the details with the center, designed a flyer, and started sending out the information. Once a few people committed to go, we invited other friends, through Facebook or emails, including many women from out of town whom we thought would benefit from this kind of retreat.

Ellen was able to schedule it on Mother's Day weekend, and titled it "Taking Time for Ourselves," offering a chance to renew and refresh before Mother's Day. We assembled a total of eight women, all local.

We began Friday night with dinner, then a get-to-know-you circle in which we shared why we had chosen to come, as well as set our intentions for the weekend.

Saturday morning began with yoga in the outdoor pavilion along the Hillsborough River, followed by breakfast and then two sessions: a presentation of photography done by one of the participants, along with some wonderful stories about each photo, and my presentation about finding balance in your life, which led to a lot of discussion and sharing. The weather was perfect, so we met on the shaded porch. I love holding classes outside!

After lunch, we had free time. I relaxed on a chaise in the enclosed porch. I had brought a book to read, but once I lay down, I was so enjoying the breeze and the bird songs that I put my book away and just closed my eyes for a bit. We met for our afternoon sessions in that same enclosed porch, so I was able to remain lying down on the chaise. One woman shared her passion for shells, another shared her favorite poem and another read from her favorite book. Ellen then led us in some breath work and meditation.

After dinner, we painted while listening to music. Some very unique, and very beautiful paintings were created. I went to bed after I finished my painting (of the landscape at the retreat center), but the others stayed up talking until almost 11 p.m.

On Sunday morning, we had breakfast and then wrote letters to ourselves to be mailed to us in a month, reminding us of our thoughts at that time. We said our goodbyes and hugged, exchanging emails so that we could stay in touch and get together again.

We went home to little responsibility, as it was Mother's Day, and most of the families had something nice planned.

It was also Derek's and Evan's ninth birthday yesterday, so we had two cakes instead of one. I ate neither one, as I still cannot eat anything sweet. But the kids didn't mind; there was more for them!

We took some pictures on their beds (a birthday tradition) and they enjoyed the present I had made for them: a photo album compilation of our Pokémon trips and adventures over the past two years.

In reflecting on the weekend, I am very pleased to have been able to stay for the whole retreat. The meditation led to a few insights, the main one being that you cannot go back to the past. Of course I know this and have been telling other people this, but I had not been giving myself the same courtesy. I had been wanting to feel emotionally as I did just before I got sick, or even during the first month I had been sick, when I still felt good but was getting incredible insight every day. As I have mentioned before, the insight is not coming as it was, and I was disappointed in that. I was just not accepting things as they are. I was reminded that I cannot possibly go back to feeling the way I did then; I can only move forward.

The retreat helped me look forward to new adventures and challenges. I realized how much I enjoy retreats and camp-like situations. I loved family camps when we attended them: meeting new people, sharing games and conversation, being out in nature, and being fed three meals a day that someone else makes! I will seek more opportunities to be in such an environment.

I also loved attending the women's retreat by myself. Granted, I did already know two women who were there, but I would have enjoyed it just as much if I had known no one. I really liked getting to know new people, and would like to find more opportunities to do so.

May 17

Put Yourself in the Picture

I have been working on an online album of the Pokémon tournaments we have attended over the past two years. It was fun looking back at how young Evan looked at age six at his first tournament, and at how excited each boy was when he won his first tournament.

I also included pictures from wherever we traveled: Georgia Aquarium, Kennedy Space Center, San Diego Zoo, Indianapolis Zoo, Hawaiian resort (we didn't get out anywhere). One thing I noticed is how few pictures of me there were. There are some, because we did think to ask people to take pictures of me with the kids. There are not many, but at least there are some.

I know many people (mostly moms) who have few to no pictures of themselves. Moms always want to take pictures of their adorable kids doing adorable things. Or they think they look fat or are not wearing a flattering shirt. Unless you are doing a fashion shoot, who cares? The point is to remember the occasion.

Moms usually take a back seat and put the focus, both photographic and otherwise, on the kids. It is the kids' choice where to go to dinner, what TV show to watch, even where to go on vacation. I give my kids a lot of say about what happens, and believe strongly in their right to choose, but only as a member of the family, not as having any more say than anyone else. Dads are often much better at expressing their opinions, and the kids learn to respect that. They eventually learn that their needs are not always going to come first.

When was the last time you did something just for yourself? Not something you had to do but something you wanted to do, maybe attend a movie or play, concert or sports game? If you have a friend to go with, great, but if not, consider going alone. If it is something you want to do, you may meet others who share your interest.

Consider putting some of the focus back on you. It probably has not been there for a long time, if ever.

May 24

Good Report

I had a check-up at the doctor today. He came in grinning and didn't stop grinning throughout the whole visit. He was very pleased with my progress, how good I am feeling, my energy level, that my hair is growing back, and that my swelling is all gone. Even when I expressed concern about the weight I had lost (seven pounds in the past month), he said *that* was a good thing! He said that had been weight from the steroids, and it needed to come off, so it is all good.

I go for another PET scan and brain MRI next month, and continue to watch and be grateful for every good day.

Next week, I am going to join the Livestrong program at the YMCA. It is a gentle exercise program for cancer survivors.

I am hopeful enough that I have planned a vacation for the end of September. A friend is hosting a get-together at the KOA campground in Williamsburg. We look forward to talking and visiting, and eating s'mores around the campfire. Cathy, our nanny, is coming along to be our driver as well as our fun-director.

Because we are going to be right there, we will extend our vacation past camping and visit Great Wolf Lodge. We first went to the one in Williamsburg four years ago, and then went the following year to the Great Wolf in the Poconos.

Great Wolf is a wonderful resort with an indoor water park that has many slides, and more importantly, MagiQuest. This is a live action quest wherein the kids have a magic wand which controls various objects in the hotel; they collect runes and experience points to move up levels. By the time we left the Poconos, the kids were all on the Leader Boards for everything they keep track of. They are quite competitive, so loved seeing their user names on the TV boards.

About a month after I got sick, Derek and I were looking at some pictures, and there was one from Great Wolf. He asked hopefully, "As soon as you are well enough, can we please plan on that being our first trip?" I am thrilled that my answer can now be "Yes!"

May 31

Mindset

Adam took a writing class a few years ago in which the students were not allowed to use the adjectives "good" or "bad" in their papers. Not only do these clichéd choices produce simplistic, boring writing, but they represent simplistic thought as well. In describing something as "good" or "bad," you are making a binary judgment.

I have written before on how it is best to suspend judgment, both of people and of situations. We do not know the full implications of a situation when it is happening, nor do we know the full measure of a person. Therefore, to judge anything as "good" or "bad" is premature and unnecessary.

Parenting books caution against labeling a child as "good" or "bad." Label the behavior itself, not the child. So rather than saying "Good boy!" when Johnny does his chores, you can say, "Thank you for emptying the dishwasher, Johnny!" And we should refrain from saying "Bad boy!" Instead say, "Johnny, the cat does not enjoy having his tail pulled."

It is important to praise the effort and work put in. Instead of saying, "You're so smart!" say "You figured those problems out!" In her book *Mindset*, Carol Dweck writes about two different modes of thought: one mode is that our ability is fixed, that we are all born with a certain level of intelligence and capability and there is really nothing one can do to change that; the other mode is that effort and motivation matter, and that while everyone is born with certain gifts and certain challenges, what we do with those is what is important.

She writes that how we react to our kids, whether telling them they are smart or pretty or athletic, matters a great deal. While they may be predisposed to believe in one mindset or the other, we can influence and modify that by our words and actions. (This is one of the only books I have cited, by the way, that I do not recommend. Some may enjoy it, but I did not like how it was written. I also found it hard to relate to the first mindset, and therefore, did not understand some of the examples.)

When we tell our children, or anyone, a judgment about them that we have made, whether positive or negative, we are implying that the trait is innate in them. While it may be lovely to hear someone tell you that you are kind, you may be more likely to feel guilty if you do an unkind act after that. You may think you have not lived up to that person's expectations of you, and may feel embarrassed. If, on the other hand, the person had said, "It was so kind of you to bring me dinner when I was sick," you have a specific idea of how you can be kind again. And while you may still think of yourself as a kind person, you may not feel you let the other person down if you do something wrong sometime too.

Of course, we want to think of ourselves as kind, compassionate, nice, etc., and there are a certain set of traits that we believe are inherent about ourselves. The question in *Mindset* is, are we able to modify those beliefs? If we believe any negative connotations about ourselves, it is even more important to realize that these traits can be changed, they are not fixed.

I believe it comes back to judgment. I was speaking with a friend last week, who was bemoaning that her daughters rarely shared much of substance regarding what happened at school that day. Rather than asking if they had a good day or even what was something good that happened, she was asking them to relate something they enjoyed that day. This helps them be in touch with their feelings, and does not call for a judgment to be made.

I shared with her how when Adam was in preschool, I used to ask him who he helped that day and how. It totally shifts the focus, and helped him look out for ways to be helpful to others, which made his days much more interesting and kind. He was able to relate actual incidents rather than just tell me he had a good day. It was a non-judgmental retelling of the day.

Watch your words. If you are using an evaluative word, you are likely making a judgment.

June 27

Great news! I had a brain MRI last week and a PET scan this week. Both are stable! It has been three months since my last scans, and it is wonderful news that my body remains stable.

We leave in a few days for the PG Retreat in Colorado Springs for a week, followed by the Pokémon Nationals in Indianapolis for a week. I am the Event Director for this year's Retreat, which has been wonderfully fulfilling, and busy. It has been a great distraction for me these past few months. And this past week there have been hundreds of emails flying back and forth as we secure last-minute plans and arrangements.

I am really looking forward to seeing this wonderful group of folks that I have the privilege of getting together with every summer. The kids love seeing their friends, and I love seeing mine!

In Indianapolis, we will have the opportunity to see different friends from across the country. Last year, there were over 1,300 players of all ages. I will get to see my brother and sister-in-law, who will join us for dinner one night.

I am grateful to be feeling well enough to carry through on my summer plans. When I booked the plane tickets back in January, I did not know what to expect or how I would be feeling. I have so much more strength and energy now that I think I may not even rest much during the trip (although I'll need to force myself to rest so that I don't overdo it!). My steroid swelling has gone away, and my hair is growing back (though in a fairly odd way—I look like I have male-pattern baldness, but have been assured that this is normal, and that it will all grow back eventually).

I have been going to the "Livestrong" program at the "Y," which is very good for me. It is slow, gentle exercise that gets the muscles working again. Everyone there is a cancer survivor, and all face their challenges, but are getting out and strengthening their bodies.

I appreciate knowing that I will be exercising with others at least twice a week. Because I draw energy from other people, just being around others is helping me improve.

I can only imagine how energized I will be after the Retreat and tournament! I really look forward to seeing everyone and sharing stories and hugs!

July 21

Vacation Report

I have come back from a wonderful world away. We were in Colorado for a week, then in Indianapolis for a week for the National Pokemon tournament. The kids had fun at the tournament and cheered on their friends who advanced to the final rounds. They played well, but none of them made top cuts. They are going to San Diego next month for the World competition, and hope to be able to play in the main event.

I will not be accompanying them to San Diego because I realized something when I was at Nationals. Although I think it is a terrific game, and I fully support their play, it is no longer *my* game. I have not kept up with the new cards that have come out in the past eight months and do not feel comfortable playing anymore. It is something that Todd shares with the boys now, as it was something I shared with them for several fun years.

I was also spoiled by the previous week away. We went to a family retreat (PG Retreat) in Colorado Springs that we have attended for six years. The organization is completely parent-run; everyone volunteers and pitches in to make it what it is. This year, I was the Event Director.

The people I see there are my people. In 2008, the first year I returned after a four-year hiatus, we had a discussion in the women's group about all going to the same nursing home when it came time, for that way, we could understand each other and share each other's lives.

It would be an amazing thing if we did not have to wait until then. This year, one dad laughingly suggested that we should all pitch in and buy the resort where we stayed so that we can live together all year long. While I don't think this is really going to happen, it is not as far-fetched as it sounds.

I have always been interested in intentional communities. When I was in high school, I wrote papers on utopian societies, and in college, I took a seminar class about them. A few years ago, after an amazing weekend camping with several friends, we talked about how great it would be if we could all live in the same neighborhood and visit each other's front porch for breakfast while the kids could play in the woods throughout the day.

There is just something fulfilling and life-affirming about being with people who understand you. At the retreat, I met some wonderful new people (about a third of the families are new each year) and almost immediately, found myself engaged in deep and meaningful conversations. This kind of deep connection is in sharp contrast to the interactions of our everyday lives. It can be very difficult to make the transition back to "normal" life. I have not generally had the problem in years past, but I did this year. Perhaps it was because this year was particularly wonderful, and I felt so appreciated for the effort I had put in throughout the year to make the retreat go as smoothly as it did. It was an emotional weekend. Jaron had warned me beforehand: "Mom, you know you're going to cry." And of course, I did. And it was very cathartic.

So now the question becomes, how does one establish those deep connections in your everyday life? I think it depends on the person with whom you are interacting, but I have certainly culled those with whom I interact to have a better chance at those deep connections. I have one friend here locally with whom I always seem to have meaningful phone conversations. We understand each other and think about things that most other people don't consider. And there are my connections from the retreat. A friend from there is one to whom I can turn about anything, and she will understand.

One thing that came up in one of the discussions at the retreat was transparency. Though everyone has different comfort levels, I have no trouble discussing my situation openly. I think this invites more real conversations because when we are open, vulnerable and transparent, hopefully others will respond in kind.

Talk about real things, real feelings and real ideas. Don't settle for superficial if you really want deep. Keep digging until you get there.

May we all be fortunate enough to have close friends in our lives. Now if we can only get that commune going!

August 20

Expansive Joy

I am very excited to share good news! I have been following a suspicious area in my lung that was first seen on a PET scan at the end of June. I spoke to a few doctors, and there was no clear direction about what to do. I had a CT scan two weeks ago, and the same area showed more suspicion; the doctors concluded it was likely tumor. But before we would schedule treatment, my doctor ordered another PET scan to see if it had changed or was stable.

I just had that PET scan, and the suspicious area is gone! It has cleared since June! I feel like dancing a jig! My friend Ellen describes this feeling as "expansive joy," when your heart just feels full.

I am so grateful that I am still going to be able to go on our planned Virginia trip—the kids and I are really looking forward to that. And I am pleased I can continue going to the gym—not only is the Livestrong program excellent, but I joined another part of it last week, which includes music and some dance moves on a chair. And I am happy that I can keep my hair! It is growing in nicely, and looks very much like it did when I was one year old (except it was blond then, and now it's brown).

The hardest part was that the doctors didn't agree on the

best course of action, so I had to weigh their recommendations, and there was no clear-cut answer. It was frustrating not knowing what to do. But now, I need to do nothing except enjoy life!

While the kids were away in New York and San Diego, I went out with friends I had not seen in months. It was great to see them in a different context than a doctor's appointment. I even went out to dinner, which I had not done since I started treatment.

Recently, I started a metaphysical movie series with a friend. We watch these deep movies and then discuss their meaning and implications. It's pretty cool.

In preparation for Jaron's upcoming Bar Mitzvah, I have been going through pictures for the slideshow. It has been very enlightening to see the progression of family relationships over the years. Not only facial expressions, but where people place themselves in the picture, who they are near, who they are holding on to…they speak volumes. A picture truly is worth a thousand words.

I also watched the video from Adam's Bar Mitzvah from two and a half years ago (which I had never watched before). Derek and Evan have grown up so much since then. I was so healthy and energetic. It will be interesting to see the dramatic changes these past few years have brought, particularly this last one. Maybe I'll even watch the video from Jaron's Bar Mitzvah before Derek and Evan have theirs!

Thanks to all of you who continue to read my updates. I know I am not posting as often as I had been. The dramatic insights have not been coming as rapidly, but perhaps that's because things have become more stable. I am very grateful to be able to think about "normal" things much of the time rather than constantly thinking about being sick and getting well.

As the new school year starts for many of you, I urge you to think just a little bit like a homeschooler. What do you want to learn about or change in your life today? It is up to you to find a way to make it happen!

September 13

Change Your Story

I have recently needed to describe myself for various online groups and sites that I have joined. As any of you who have tried this before know, it is difficult! How do you define yourself? What aspects of your personality or lifestyle do you emphasize? How do you convey your essence in a short paragraph?

Whereas in the past I would have begun any description with "A homeschool mom," that is no longer my primary self-image. I am still working on a new definition.

Our main roles change over time: daughter, student, friend, wife, parent, teacher, mentor, community leader, cancer patient, survivor. Our characteristics change and evolve, depending upon where we choose to focus: helper, supporter, recipient of help, offerer of insight.

In *Redirect*, Timothy Wilson offers many examples of "story editing." His research found that much of what makes social programs successful involves helping participants redefine themselves: from at-risk youth to indispensible friend; from juvenile delinquent to valued community helper. He showed that explaining traumatic events in a new way can dramatically reduce post-traumatic stress disorder, that just reliving and talking about what happened does not help, but that creating a new story about what happened does help.

Story editing even helps students who initially received a poor grade on a college exam. Those students who interpreted the grade as proof that college was too hard and maybe they weren't really "college material" had poorer grades throughout their college career (if they even remained in college). Those students who instead were told that many students do poorly initially, but with improved study habits, excel, increased their grades almost immediately and kept the higher grades throughout the four years. This reflects the idea I described a while ago, as outlined in *Mindset*: that ability is not fixed; rather, effort makes a difference.

How do we think of ourselves? Many people beat themselves up and do not treat themselves kindly. Whenever anything goes wrong, they attribute it to something in themselves that is unchangeable. Those who are more resilient instead see setbacks as temporary and circumstantial. This is not the same as blaming someone else for your problems.

The billboards that proclaim, "Injured? Someone should pay!" do not lead to a responsible citizenry. But if you spill a glass of milk, you can think, "I'm clumsy" or you can think, "The glass was slippery." The former may lead to feeling bad about yourself, whereas the latter lets you know that next time, you can wipe off the glass and be less likely to spill.

Viewing yourself as a competent individual is much more beneficial than viewing life as out to get you. In *Flourish*,

Martin Seligman discusses techniques that people can use to help themselves lead more fulfilling lives. First among these is keeping a gratitude journal. Second is focusing on our character strengths and amplifying those, rather than focusing on our weaknesses or flaws. Seligman, a founder of the Positive Psychology movement, also found that meaning and engagement (long-term satisfaction) in one's life and one's community are key components to happiness, along with pleasurable experiences (short-term satisfaction).

I have written before about engaging in your community and building a community of your own. Meaning in your life has to do with recognizing and building on your particular strengths and feeling that you are making a difference in the world, in whatever way works for you.

Increasing your pleasurable experiences harks back to much of what I have written about before: focusing on your senses and calming your mind, slowing down and appreciating every moment Seligman calls this savoring.

To help you define your strengths, as well as learn more about optimism and other aspects of happiness, visit *authentichappiness.com*.

A pillar of the Gifted community, Stephanie Tolan explains story editing in her e-book, "Change Your Story, Change Your Life," which is available to download free at *storyhealer.com*. Tolan believes that stories have the power to help with healing. How will you change your story?

October 27

It's never too late for closet right-brainers to free themselves from the shackles of convention for the boundless exploits of the unfamiliar.
—Right Brain Terrain

Perhaps I really am a closet right-brainer. I always thought of myself as classically left-brained: organized, logical and sequential. But there is a creative and free side which I want to explore.

This past weekend, I was fortunate enough to go to Camp Living Springs, a camp for cancer survivors. There were 75 campers and 25 volunteers. While everyone was there for the same reason, we did not have scheduled activities where we discussed cancer. Sure, over the course of talking with people, cancer came up and everyone shared their stories. But when we all introduced ourselves, we were asked to say our name, where we grew up, and what our favorite job had been. We were not asked what type of cancer we had or how long we had been done with treatment. It was an important distinction.

The first night, there was a karaoke singer. When people wanted to sing, they did; otherwise, he sang. The reason I say I may be a right-brainer is that I sang karaoke for the first time, and I loved it! I sang with a woman I had just met who had also never done karaoke before. While we were both a bit nervous, I told her that there was no better opportunity than that moment; we were surrounded by the most supportive, encouraging group of people that we probably ever would find. We sang "Kodachrome" by Paul Simon, and everyone cheered.

The rest of the night, the singer played dance music, and I danced to every song. I had not danced that much in twenty years. It was great fun!

To everyone that I met at camp, I was "the girl who loves to dance and sing." What a great persona to have; what a great way to be known. It was an amazing experience to be able to invent yourself exactly as you wish to be. I was myself, just a particular part of myself, that was really fun and carefree. I loved it.

There are a few opportunities we have in life to do this. When you go to a new school, or off to college, or to a new job, or relocate to a new city, you can be exactly who you want to be, either consciously or unconsciously. I did not consciously decide to be a fun person when I went to camp; I just followed my bliss by dancing and singing, and discovered a part of myself that had lain dormant for many years, or had never come out at all.

When I started high school, I knew no one. I was starting over, and on that first day, in homeroom, we filled out an index card with our name. Up to that point, I had been Lannie, short for Elanna. People mispronounced my name all the time, so I decided to do something about it. On that index card, I wrote Loni. No one has mispronounced my name since. Along with that small change, I realized I could be whoever I chose to be. When I was fourteen, I don't think I consciously chose too many details, but who knows? I may have.

I found the quote above on a manifesto on a website called *Right Brain Terrain*. I just love the idea of "freeing yourself from the shackles of convention for the boundless exploits of the unfamiliar."

I am ready for those exploits of the unfamiliar. Anyone else want to come along for the ride?

November 10

Bar Mitzvah!

Jaron's Bar Mitzvah was last weekend. Thanks to those of you who were able to join us; I will have pictures for those of you who weren't.

It was a wonderful weekend: lots of family members came, the kids enjoyed visiting with their cousins, I enjoyed visiting with my cousins, and everyone got along.

And Jaron? He did a great job. His voice is beautiful, and he appreciated hearing everyone say so. Hopefully he will have many more opportunities to share his prowess, now that he realizes how much he enjoys singing for others.

The whole experience was very much as you might expect for a second-born child: just as nice, and everything got done, just as it did for the first, but without the stress and anxiety that you encounter the first time around. I was very relaxed about the whole thing; I didn't even know what I was wearing until that day. And thankfully, everything just fell into place.

Thanks to Todd's mom for coordinating the family brunch on Sunday. And thanks to our caterers, photographer and DJ for providing such a warm atmosphere at the tent reception on Saturday night. The layout was lovely, and we got to dance! I even went up in the chair after Jaron did.

I am so grateful to have been able to fully participate in this special day.

Before I got sick, we had not yet chosen a date for Jaron's Bar Mitzvah. We knew it would be sometime after his birthday (he was thirteen in September) due to the high holidays, but thought we might even wait until the spring. Once I started treatment, we chose the earliest possible date after his birthday, and Rabbi told me that if need be, we could move the date up further. I am fortunate that we did not have to change a thing, and I was able to joyously celebrate this milestone with Jaron.

I would like to share with you all the speech I gave at his Bar Mitzvah. He had tears in his eyes as I spoke.

Wow, Jaron. All the work you put in clearly paid off. You have done such a beautiful job; your voice is uplifting and your singing gave us all a more spiritual experience.

When it came time to begin preparation for your Bar Mitzvah, Zadie drove you to meet with the Rabbi, and often sat in on your sessions. Both you and he really enjoyed these excursions, as you listened to old music, stopped for lunch and made a few side trips to interesting places to explore. Rabbi commented on your interaction with Zadie that "every kid should be lucky enough to have such a relationship with their grandparent: more of a friendship with a great deal of mutual respect."

You enjoyed reading with Zadie, and though he may not be able to carry a tune, he did help teach you some of the prayers. You were a willing student, and found that you actually enjoyed the preparation much more than you thought you would.

You were the happiest child I have ever seen. Your preschool teacher, Ms. Pat, used to talk about how you would sit contentedly on the floor, doing a puzzle, singing. You were always smiling, laughing, singing.

Your name, Jaron, means to sing, and we could not have picked a more apt name for you. Though you may not have been looking forward to your Bar Mitzvah preparation initially, you have thoroughly enjoyed it because you have had the opportunity to work with wonderful people, and because you have had a chance to sing.

When I think of all the different things you have been passionate about, most share the common theme of creativity. From acting to Irish Step Dancing, 3-D puzzles to origami, soft pastel hummingbirds to anime, pesto to marble cheesecake, you pour yourself into your creations.

You are incredibly protective of your brothers. There are many pictures of you with your arms draped, not across their shoulders, but across their chests. You shield them from harm and hurt, while being their teacher, their mentor, their brother, their friend.

Whether making a meal for them or playing a computer game, you are there for them.

With Adam, you share a sense of humor for the absurdities in life, as well as a love of games. Together, you created some wonderful versions of "Ticket To Ride," with him writing the cards and you drawing the maps.

When you were four, you cried at the beauty of a rainbow, and you cried because you understood that the sun would not always exist. But the rest of the time, you were happy. Smiling, laughing, full of joy.

Last year, we went to the National Gallery of Art together. You showed me things in the paintings I never would have seen. You pointed out colors and brush strokes: details that an artist notices, but a lay person does not. You taught me how to see.

You taught me how to draw. I never became any good at it, but you patiently explained how to use color and shading and gently corrected how I held the pencil. Later, you taught homeschool art classes to your friends, demonstrating the same ability to pass on your technique.

You bring such positive energy to a room. As Evan explained it when you were away in New York this summer, "When Jaron is here, everything is in color. And when he's gone, it's in black and white."

When I got sick last year, you stepped up as you always do. You cooked meals for your brothers, helped Bubbie shop and keep up the house and helped maintain as much normalcy as possible for the family. When friends were kind enough to have you kids over, you watched over Derek and Evan in my place. I never worried about them when you were along.

I am so grateful that I have been able to count on you. Now that you are officially a man, expect that to increase. (LOL!) Don't worry...I know you can handle it!

In his famous speech, "Never Give Up," Jim Valvano said this:

"To me, there are three things we all should do every day. We should do this every day of our lives. Number one is laugh. You should laugh every day. Number two is think. You should spend some time in thought. And number three is, you should have your emotions moved to tears, could be happiness or joy. But think about it. If you laugh, you think, and you cry, that's a full day. That's a heck of a day. You do that seven days a week, you're going to have something special."

You do these three things naturally, and have almost every day of your life. I am so proud of who you are and who you will become.

November 11

Adam's Bar Mitzvah was two and a half years ago. I would like to share the speech I gave:

Wow. We are so proud of you. You did an amazing job here today, and last night. In addition to the preparation you did for your Bar Mitzvah today, you have been working on a project which will be the theme of this evening's reception: your family tree.

I love that you chose to connect your Bar Mitzvah with all the generations that have come before you through researching your ancestors and the stories surrounding them.

Though your current interest in genealogy was sparked by an assignment in a homeschool class I taught last year, your fascination with the subject goes back much farther.

I have a family tree you scrawled when you were six, just after Derek and Evan were born. And when you were four, you used to write out the birth and death years of people, both real and imagined.

This connection to and interest in roots and history, not just your own, is, I believe, yet another reason why you love to play bridge.

When you sit down at a bridge table, you get the wonderful benefit of looking beyond the cards to the other people sitting across from you. You have played against corporate CEOs, history professors and professional bridge players. You have also played against the grandma who lives next door. And you have treated each one with courtesy and respect. These older folks have an amazing storehouse of experience that they readily and happily share with you. I will always be grateful to Jim for making you into as much of a grammar stickler as I am. And I know you get a kick out of listening to Led Zeppelin while hearing tales of great Italian restaurants. Ruth and Bob, who first taught you bridge when you were five, have maintained a close relationship through frequent visits. They have expanded your horizons as they share tales of all the amazing places they have visited around the world.

All the bridge players you have had the privilege of knowing help connect you to the past, while you help connect them to the future.

You have always had a particularly close relationship with all your grandparents. The long walks you used to take with Zadie, listening to all his stories lent a special bond to your relationship, as evidenced by his presence here next to you on the Bema today. While Bubbie used to sing you "This Old Man" to help you fall asleep when you were little, your relationship has evolved as she now looks forward to accompanying you on more bridge tournaments as your chaperone.

The highlight of your past three or four summers, has been your extended stay in New York at Grandma and

Grandpa's house. Not only did you get the freedom away from your parents and brothers, but also the fun with your uncles, aunts and cousins. The endless card games with Grandma and Grandpa until all hours of the night included Hearts, gin and poker.

The only note of sadness in the joy of today is that Grandpa could not be here with us to see you reach this milestone. He was always so proud of you, and I know he would have been especially proud of you today.

As you were researching your family tree, you delighted in hearing the stories and making the connections. You were able to trace back over seven generations, to the early 1800s. In searching for your past, you are learning about your place in the future. I trust that you will continue to cherish your Jewish heritage and pass that heritage on to your children.

Though you may have the skepticism of a teenager, you often demonstrate the insight of an adult. You have observed that Judaism makes sense, ethically and morally. I know that you will build upon that foundation to become the person we all know you can be.

You have grown into such a kind, funny, thoughtful, responsible young man who is such a joy to be with. Dad and I are so proud of you.

November 25

Almost Exactly One Year Ago...

Just prior to Thanksgiving, I completed two Cyberknife treatments for a lesion in my brain. I had five spots that remained after my treatment (after about 15 original spots) and we have just been watching them. They have either remained stable or shrunk over the course of six months. One spot became active in September, so we explored different options and chose the Cyberknife.

Cyberknife is focused radiation delivered by a robotic arm like the one they use to build cars. It takes a picture every second and then delivers its radiation blast. Very high-tech! Two hour-long treatments, and I was done.

This is a very strange week for me, as it was exactly one year ago that I was diagnosed. It was the Monday after Thanksgiving that I went in the hospital. How very grateful I am to be recalling this milestone. What a year it has been!

I am celebrating my year with a trip to Sedona, Arizona. I went there about twenty years ago, and thought it was beautiful and peaceful. In trying to decide where to go, something drew me there. I'll let you all know upon my return what it was! I will take excursions to the Grand Canyon, ancient ruins and an energy vortex, along with just enjoying the scenery.

December 18

First, a Medical Update:

Just before Thanksgiving, I had the Cyberknife treatment for two spots in my brain. It went very well…the MRI of my brain from last week showed exactly what it was supposed to show after treatment. I had a PET scan the week before that, and it was all clear as well. I am very thankful for such great results.

When I went to the oncology office for a follow up visit, the nurses cheered with me about finishing my first year as a survivor. For that is the definition of the American Cancer Society: You become a survivor the day you are diagnosed, and keep it going from there.

Now, the Fun Stuff:

My trip to Sedona was a lot of fun. It snowed two of the days: one day, I was at the Grand Canyon and the other, in Sedona itself. I did get to the Grand Canyon while it was still clear, so I got to see the view before it was obscured. I went on a bus tour, and we walked around for about an hour on our own.

I went on a Pink Jeep Tour to Broken Arrow Trail. I had never been in a jeep before. I was sitting in the very back seat, so whenever the driver went on a downward slant, my seat belt was the only thing holding me in my seat. It was very rugged, and when we went by some cliff areas, my heart was in my throat. But we saw some beautiful areas that I never could have gotten to on my own, and had a very knowledgeable guide who taught us all about the trees and plants indigenous to the desert.

Sedona is famous for its energy vortexes. I set up a private session with a woman who specializes in this area, and we went to two different sites to feel the energy, meditate, let go of the past and look forward to the future.

For two days, I walked around Sedona and the surrounding artists' community. They had beautiful and unique collections there. I had fun shopping for some special gifts.

One night, the mayor lit the town Christmas tree. The revelers huddled under the shop awnings to stay out of the falling snow. But what a beautiful backdrop it made! There were carolers, and hot chocolate with cookies. It felt like Bedford Falls! Such a quaint small town. There was one man who dressed in a cowboy hat and boots, and even wore a holster with a gun. He looked like an extra in a Western movie. I later found out that he was like the town mascot; he greeted visitors as he wandered the streets. There was a newspaper article about him in one of the shops. Quite a character!

My first day in Arizona, I had breakfast with a friend from PG Retreat who lives in Phoenix. I love knowing people across the country and being able to catch up with friends from whom it feels you were never apart. This is another benefit of having found my tribe; we have much in common even if we don't know each other well. Conversation flows easily and comfortably whenever we come together.

My Next Trip:

The day after Christmas, I am going to Winter Dance Week at the John Campbell Folk School in Brasstown, North Carolina. Another friend from PG Retreat recommended this school, which holds classes in arts, crafts, music and dance. We will be learning contra, square, English country, Morris, Rapper Sword and Scandinavian Couples Dancing. I have only ever done the first two, but as I wrote before, I re-discovered that I really love to dance, so I thought this was a perfect fit.

Last week, I found several outfits at the thrift store, so I am ready to go!

Revelations to Share:

Following the Livestrong Program at the Y (which I am still doing as a drop-in), there is a class called Transitions, which is designed to help you with "Life After Cancer." There is nutrition, exercise, medical management, and emotional support. About a month ago, we were talking about life plans, and I commented that I felt I did not have the right to plan anything six months from now.

As I have said before, when you are in treatment, and following, you are so focused on the moment that it is hard to think beyond your next doctor's appointment. It is also really hard because you just have no idea of what is going to happen. Of course, no one knows what is going to happen, but once you have that cancer diagnosis hanging over your head, you have a stronger sense of not knowing what the future may hold. Despite all the positive thoughts and beliefs, there is an underlying sense that your future is not in your hands.

Again, this is true for everyone, but it is in the forefront once you have that diagnosis. So I felt that I could not legitimately plan for something months away, because I just didn't know how I would be at that time. However, the others in the group shared their experiences, as well as an understanding of what I meant. They told me I did have the right to plan. I thought about it, but I did not believe it until after my trip to Sedona and my most recent clear scans.

As with so much else, it is not even that I thought it through and know that it is logically true that I can plan. It is just a clarity, a knowing that I can.

In watching a documentary on the Chautauqua Institute, I was reminded that taking classes there one summer was something I have always wanted to do. So I am going to do it. I already have my hotel booked for next July and am so excited!

While it is still true that I do not know what the future holds, none of us do, and it is no reason not to plan. What I do know now is not to wait. If it is something you want to do and can do, do it. Do not wait.

The Cancer Camp that I went to in October allows you to attend twice. In speaking with one of the other campers this year, I said that I plan to come back next year. He said he thought maybe he'd wait a year and not return right away. I say, "Why wait?" If you know you want to, and you know you can, just do it!

January 16, 2012

I Hope You Dance

"There are shortcuts to happiness. And dancing is one of them."
—Dance website

I have never been an athlete. Sure, I was on the gymnastics team in seventh grade, but I worked hard to master the basics. I did Israeli dancing for a few years, and I did love that, but it seemed more like a physical expression of spirit (like yoga). Before I got to high school, I learned from my brother that if you are the manager for the basketball team (keeping stats), you don't have to take PE. So I was the manager for the girls' basketball team, and I got the experience of traveling to away games and never having to break a sweat.

So imagine my surprise when what intrigued and enticed me for my winter vacation was a Dance Week in the mountains of North Carolina. Todd took the kids on a cruise with his family, so I had about ten days on my own. Adam and I were home for the first few days; I got a chance to ride in the car with him driving and didn't flinch once! But I digress. I asked friends for suggestions of someplace cool to go where I could learn something, or just go to a beautiful place and do something cool. A friend recommended John C. Campbell Folk School in Brasstown, North Carolina. My friend and her daughter do contra dancing, and she said this was a place she had always wanted to go.

They have Winter Dance Week between Christmas and New Year's. I had contra danced twice before: once at family camp in New Hampshire, about four years ago, and once locally following that. I thought it was great fun, but had not continued it because the spinning made me dizzy. I had square danced once about ten years ago when our babysitter at the time brought me and my father to share her avocation. It was a lot of fun also, but I never went back.

Before deciding to go to the dance camp, I called to ensure that I could get a cabin close to the dance hall and the dining hall. With reassurances that the camp administrators would do all they could to help me, I registered. Upon arrival, I was taken to a cabin far from the main area. When I went to the office and explained my situation, they switched me immediately to the closest lodging, which was a recently renovated single room with a private bath and a spectacular view. Sometimes being less than 100 percent well has its benefits.

I was delighted to find a mix of ages, fairly balanced male-female ratio, and as a group, some of the most interesting, intelligent, well-spoken and kind people I have ever met. There was a full range of dance experience, and the more well-versed happily taught those of us who were new to it all. This kind of dancing is very democratic: you have a different partner for each dance, so you learn a variety of techniques from each partner. Though a few suggestions were contradictory, the majority of them built upon each other, so that by the end of the first night, I was pretty clear on most of the calls. During each class and before each dance, the callers explained new or complicated moves and rehearsed them with us. And most of the time, I was dancing with a more experienced partner who helped guide me through each move if I didn't get it. Though it took a few rounds, I would usually get it right well before the end of the dance.

And boy, did it feel good when it clicked. It was like my body just knew what to do. I imagine one would get the same feeling playing an instrument and mastering a piece, the flow when your body gets it, and just does each move without you consciously telling it every step of the way. I felt so empowered, so invigorated, so competent. What a tremendous feeling! I knew I was doing well when some of the more experienced men asked me to dance and shared more advanced tips. And two wonderful gentlemen taught me how to waltz. They were so gracious.

We ate our meals family style, and were encouraged to rotate tables to meet everyone. I was pleased to discuss real topics, real ideas, real opinions. By the end of the week, two or three people that I had gotten to know quite well knew about my cancer. But no one else had any idea. More knew that I homeschooled my four boys, but even that was a fairly small number. I was simply someone who had come to dance. And was doing so five or six hours every day. I was no more tired than anyone else.

The energy and spirit I drew from the group was invigorating.

The last night of camp was New Year's Eve. I shared some touching moments with a some people who had become good friends (New Year's Eve is an emotional time for many). The last morning, I made plans with a few people to join them at another dance week in August in Massachusetts. I am excited to have that planned.

A dear friend who lives in Tennessee took me to the airport following camp. It was a great transition away from the high of dancing constantly, as well as a great chance to catch up.

Upon returning home, I searched for dance venues nearby. The closest is about 45 minutes away. But I went there the first weekend I was home, and introduced a friend to contra. She loved it so much that she plans to go back with me next month and bring her daughter to try it too. I hope anyone else who lives near me might consider going. It's a great activity that you can attend alone, or with someone. It's great exercise and great fun, and you feel so proud when you master a move!

I just read an article about how great dancing is for staving off mental decline. The researchers hypothesize that it is the split-second decisions you need to make in dance, in responding to your partner and adjusting as necessary, that keep the mind sharp. Anything to increase acuity sounds great to me.

Another thing I found was that I was working in concert with my body rather than separately from it. I am so used to living in my head and having my body come along for the ride. It was nice to have my body driving for a while. I found it similar to when I realized a year and a half ago that I needed to follow my heart instead of my head. It is nice to give my head a break sometimes.

I am so glad I chose to go to dance week. It opened up a whole new world for me, and again reinforced, "Don't postpone joy."

January 27, 2012

School?

While I was dancing in North Carolina, Todd was on the annual Kaplan cruise with the kids. Perhaps prompted by conversations there, Jaron decided he wants to go to school in the fall. He is going to attend a homeschool co-op next semester, so he will interact with many more kids than he has done in the past, but he feels it will not be enough. He also feels he is ready to "get serious about his schoolwork." He has taken marine biology online, and is currently taking algebra online. He enjoys these classes, but is longing for the classroom interaction with both teacher and students.

When Todd told me that Jaron had made that decision, he also told me that he wanted Derek and Evan to go to school in the fall as well. My immediate reaction was feeling as if I had been kicked in the gut. I could not believe that Derek and Evan would even be open to the idea of going to school (especially Evan, who once told me he would rather live in Antarctica than go to school). I could not believe that our idyllic homeschool life might be coming to an end.

Todd saw how upset I was, and explained that he was supportive of homeschooling for Adam because he was clearly not going to fit in school. While he saw that homeschool was the right fit for Adam, he was never convinced of its merits for the others. He felt they would do perfectly fine in school, as they did not have many of the issues that Adam had, and would be more likely to succeed in the "normal" environment of school. He wanted them to try. I was not convinced until he gave me his last reason: that if there came a point when I was no longer able to homeschool them, wouldn't it be better for me to have already helped them adjust to school rather than them having to adjust without me there to support them? I again felt kicked in the gut, but I knew he was right. Just as our job as parents is to ease our kids into the real world, to help them reach independence and work ourselves out of a job, my job educationally was to ensure that they would be stable and secure in a school environment, for there might come a day when they would have to go with that option.

We agreed when I first got sick that it would have been way too traumatic to place them in school along with their mother having just been diagnosed with cancer, after having moved out of the house and then moving back in. We agreed that we should try to minimize any additional changes at that time, especially the stress of going to school for the first time. Now, all of a sudden, that was changing. Granted, it had been a year since my diagnosis and it was no longer an acute situation. I was feeling good and could explore all options with them. I felt Todd was right that it was important for me to be there to help them navigate the world of school, so instead of them having to go when it was a crisis situation, it was better for them to go in the fall, when I could help them every step of the way.

When we talked to Derek and Evan about it, Derek said he wasn't happy about it, but would do whatever we need him to. Evan said he did not want to, but would investigate further.

Since school choice is coming up in February, we will take the next month to visit all the schools under consideration. This will hopefully give us all more of a sense of control about their going to school. Fortunately, Ms. Cathy is still with us, and can help get them prepped for more school-like work. She has always been willing to take on the tasks that I dread, and this is one of those tasks. We will work on their handwriting and Evan's reading skills. We will have weekly spelling lists with tests. We will try to prepare them as much as we can to be ready for school.

I am saddened by the idea of no longer homeschooling, but I know that in my heart, and hopefully in their hearts, we will always be homeschoolers.

March 6

Creating Memories

How do you want the snapshots of you to turn out? The one who is turned away, scowling, grousing, complaining, or worst of all, not even there? Or smiling, laughing, joyous, enjoying the occasion and being a part of it? No matter how large or small a **part you play, at least be there so you can be in the picture.**

Some people make it a policy to always come to celebrate the happy occasions, but far too many people will make it to a funeral, yet skip a birthday party or even a wedding. I admit I missed my fair share of Bar Mitzvahs, though rarely a wedding. Now that I am feeling able to, I have made it my policy to always be there for the good things: I want to take every opportunity to celebrate life.

My cousin's son got married in Philadelphia this past weekend, and I had the good fortune to attend this joyous ceremony. It was unlike any wedding I have ever attended before. The bride and groom were celebrated as a king and queen, entertained and honored throughout the day. Though this is not unusual in traditional Judaism, I had never been a participant before.

Something Extraordinary

There was much dancing and singing, poetry, jokes, stories, toasts, juggling, unicycling, and even sword swallowing. Despite the 200-plus guests, it felt warm and intimate.

There were family I had not seen in five to fifteen years, family friends I had not seen in thirty years, and some relatives I had never met. All were welcomed with open arms, kindly and graciously.

As I looked around the room at those who were there, and thought of those who weren't, I was especially glad I had come. Years from now, when someone mentions this wedding weekend, I hope they will remember that I was there and that my presence helped make the occasion that much more memorable. I not only want to have my own memories, but want to be in other people's memories.

I have written before about putting yourself in the picture, and finding ways to have experiences and make memories. In speaking with my cousin's husband, he mentioned that he was looking forward to seeing my dad at the wedding. He said a lovely thing about my dad: Ira knows how to make memories. He shared that his kids still fondly remember my dad's visit to them when they lived in Puerto Rico and my dad let the kids bury him in the sand. A small gesture, an afternoon's fun, yet over 15 years later, when his kids think of Uncle Ira, they picture him up to his neck in San Juan sand.

I thought back to different times with my dad, and similar snapshots emerged: going on a Sunday drive to the country after visiting the flea market and buying a small china animal, playing with his talis during long hours of Yom Kippur services, helping him shine his shoes, dancing with him this weekend and discovering he is quite a dancer! He is good at making memories, because he is good at making things fun. My kids share similar recollections, as he has graced us with months of his company for many winters now.

Of course these are wonderful memories for my father to have, but even more so, these are memories that those around him have, and will continue to have once he is no longer able to make more.

They say you live on in the memories of those you leave behind. In Judaism, when you speak of someone who has died, you say, "May his memory be a blessing." So be sure and be out there, making memories not just for yourself, but for those around you, even those you didn't know you impacted. They will remember, and you will live on.

May 18

Choosing a School, and Vice Versa

We have been busy these last few months focusing on the upcoming launch into school. I visited several schools with Jaron, including a private school that we had heard rave reviews about that both of us thought felt aesthetically like a prison, one that we both liked which was very outdoor-oriented, and his zoned school where he shadowed for the day in the gifted program. While the zoned school seemed fine, everyone he met told him not to go there. They told him he should go anywhere but there. He did school choice for the school we liked, but did not get placed via the lottery. He was faced with his zoned middle school, or perhaps another option.

I had spoken with him about the possibility of just going straight to high school, because I thought that no one should go to middle school unless absolutely necessary! He thought going to eighth grade would be better because it would give him a year to adjust to school without the grades counting for college. I thought ninth grade would be a better fit socially because several schools would be converging into one, and not everyone would know each other, as they would in eighth grade.

When the eighth grade guidance counselor was registering him, she saw his test scores (I satisfied Florida's minimal homeschooling requirements by administering an individual achievement test, the Woodcock-Johnson, to the kids each year). She called and offered that he could skip eighth grade and go directly to ninth. Her call prompted a reconsideration of the best placement. I called the high school and scheduled an appointment with a guidance counselor. What a pleasure it was to return to Gulf High with Jaron, where I had been a guidance counselor before Adam was born. A few of the counselors and the secretary were the same lovely folks I had worked with 17 years ago. After speaking with us, they recommended that Jaron try the International Baccalaureate (IB) program for ninth grade. They thought it would be the program of best fit for him, and he agreed. I think it may be a challenge, but it will be a great opportunity for him to have the more formal schoolwork he longs for while being surrounded by other really smart kids from across the county. I am excited for him.

Derek, Evan and I visited several schools, including the elementary campus of the private school Jaron and I had visited. The classes were too small and the setting was arid. We visited a school with a huge playground that Derek was excited about, but it did not offer a gifted program. We visited the other gifted program aside from their zoned school, and thought the school grounds were beautiful: green and lush with gardens and fields. Unfortunately, when we observed the fifth grade gifted classroom, we saw a teacher who had no control over her classroom teaching a lesson about science and food chains that Derek and Evan had learned when they were four years old.

Finally, I visited their zoned school and was allowed to observe the fifth grade gifted teacher. The boys, however, were not allowed to come ("School policy!" Ugh!). I was so impressed by the teacher that it was enough for all of us. He taught an interesting lesson, fluidly moved between many students in turn, and seemed like he respected his students and engendered respect from them. I thought he would be a great fit for them. When I asked for an opportunity for Derek and Evan to observe the class, I was told that we could come during an open house when the students would have their country projects on display. We went and met the teacher. He seemed like a no-nonsense teacher with great control of his classroom, which is exactly what they need. (The question they asked at every school we visited, aside from if they had to learn cursive, was "What do you do about bullying?")

While Evan is still miserable at the thought of going to school, going through this process of visiting several schools and discussing and ranking the pros and cons of each, has put the focus onto "Where are we going to school?" rather than "Are we going to school?" This has helped tremendously in accepting that this is going to happen in a few months.

In the meantime, we have gotten Evan a tutor for reading and writing. His tutor comes twice a week, and she has honed in on exactly what his problems have been. As soon as she had him syllabify words, miraculously, he could spell. And as soon as he read with a guide paper to block any text below the line he was reading, his reading speed doubled. He does have some issues, but I no longer believe he has dyslexia, just some learning differences that can be remediated with intense one-on-one help by someone he enjoys working with. His self-esteem is climbing as he sees what he is capable of doing. What a joy!

We have everything in place for the three younger kids to go to school in the fall. Adam will continue with his community college classes along with bridge tournaments squeezed in between. He is looking forward to his first English class after several years of taking only math. When we were looking for which professor to select, we read on one of the Christian homeschool group's websites to stay away from one professor because he assigned controversial books and discussed controversial topics during class. Adam read that and said, "Sign me up!" I think he will love it! A few years ago, we participated in a homeschool book club. We chose our books from the Banned Books Reading List. Adam reveled in being able to discuss these books openly with like-minded teens and adults. I imagine this class will offer something similar. He is so ready for that kind of intellectual challenge and heady discussion.

I continue to homeschool as I have, trying to squeeze in the last few months before we enter the new world of public school. It shall be an interesting exercise.

June 16

Words to Live By

It has been three months since my last update. Thankfully, no news really is good news.

I have had stable or shrinking lesions on my scans, and have been feeling great. I pulled my hip flexor muscle back in February, so was grounded from the gym and dancing for months, but have been taking an anti-inflammatory these past few weeks and am able to move about more freely now.

I continue to be grateful for the good health to which I wake each day.

Last week, I had the honor of being interviewed by a friend who does genealogy studies and records people's life stories. It was fun thinking of some things from childhood—what and who I remembered. We haven't finished the interview yet, so I have not yet had a chance to expound on my philosophy of life, but I did prepare for that. It was really not hard—there are but a few aphorisms that I try to live by and would like my kids to adopt and remember.

I have shared many of them in past entries, but will repeat a few here:

Do the Right Thing

I have always said this to my kids when they are wavering or unsure of what to do or how to do it. It is clear and simple, and while there are times when the right thing is not obvious, your gut knows 90 percent of the time. Follow it.

Let It Go

I have written about this before. I just read a list of "Signs of Spiritual Awakening" that includes loss of interest in conflict, loss of interest in worrying, loss of interest in judging, and loss of interest in interpreting the actions of others. It is not up to me to think about why or what someone has done. Assume good intent.

I'm on Your Side

This was my grandfather's favorite thing to say. We always knew it was true, and it was a great comfort to know we were not alone. It gives you strength to know someone is always in your corner. My kids know I have their back and will always support them, even if I don't agree with them.

Wonderful, Most Wonderful

This is a great phrase I learned from our esteemed storyteller at PG Retreat. She told the fable of the farmer whose son broke his leg, which some might look upon as tragic, yet it spared him from going into the army and being killed. There is much more to the story, but the point is that the farmer always looked at each event that happened as "Wonderful, most wonderful," no matter how bad it seemed at the time. For in the end, it all did turn out to be most wonderful.

I have felt that way all along with my cancer, and as I pass each milestone, I look back and I see the good in every step of the way. Which leads to the last one:

It's All Good

I say this all the time. And it's true. It's the whole optimism thing, but if you look at it in all aspects of your life, it will help you be a much calmer and happier person. It helps you remember to breathe.

We are being visited this weekend by a documentary film crew that is shooting a movie about bridge and how to revitalize the game. Its working title is "Lost in the Shuffle." It is great fun sharing our lives with them. They ask terrific questions, and we get to talk about what we do, what we think. After spending a few hours with us, the director got tears in his eyes as he said, "I just realized what this story is really all about. It's about the relationship between Mom and the kids, and how that affects their education, bridge, all of it." It was so cool to have someone get it so quickly. Everything comes down to relationships.

Derek and Evan met the teacher they are going to have in the fall. He is dynamic, funny, and attuned to each individual child. We were all greatly relieved and excited at the relationship they will have and the support that is inherent in a strong bond with a good teacher.

Evan has been working with a tutor over the past several months, and has recently switched to a second one for the summer. Each of them taught him a simple technique that dramatically improved his spelling and his reading fluency. He is much happier now and more confident in all areas. Evan's new favorite activity is writing in Greek. I discovered the Greek font for a project Jaron was doing, and Evan thought it was fantastic. He writes sentences and stories using the Greek font, and asks us to read what he wrote. Jaron does very well, since he learned the Greek alphabet. I can read most of it, and Derek is learning.

I have discovered Khan Academy. I knew about it a year ago, but we just started using it about a month ago. It is absolutely amazing. Derek and Evan have each filled in their elementary math and beyond. Evan loves figuring out angle measures and logic. Jaron has been watching art history videos. Adam learned a year of high school chemistry in a week to pass a college exam to get into an upper-level college chemistry class. Khan is how learning should be: everyone can focus on what he is interested in and delve deeply into it, with a gentle guide along the way.

I had great fun with trivia and karaoke these past few months. A hotel five minutes from my house hosted these events, and I met different groups of friends there each time. Jaron accompanied me sometimes as well, and we always had a great time. It was nice having a fun place to go every Friday night, and since I never knew who would show up, it was, again, "like a box of chocolates" to open the door and see which friends were there.

Summer is rapidly approaching. We are traveling quite a bit. Adam is traveling the most, as usual: Colorado (PGR), Seattle, cruise to Alaska, Philadelphia (bridge), and finally, China, to represent the U.S. in bridge, as he did in Turkey and Croatia over the last few years. The others are going to Indianapolis (Pokémon nationals—Derek only), Colorado (PGR), Seattle, cruise to Alaska, and Michigan (Yunasa camp—Jaron and Derek). While they are cruising to Alaska, I will be in New York visiting a dear friend from high school in Ithaca, then off to Chautauqua, to learn and be enriched. In August, I go to Massachusetts for another dance camp.

A note of sadness just before we leave for Colorado: our dear, wonderful nanny, Cathy, who has been with us for over ten years, will be leaving. Because we will be traveling so much and then the kids are headed to school, we are going to try it without her. She has been such a huge part of our lives, and such a tremendous support and teacher for us all. We will miss her dearly. But she has promised to stay in touch and have dinner once a month with one or more of the kids. And she is just a phone call away. And it will be wonderful, most wonderful…

August 30

End-of-Summer Update

It has been a marvelous summer: lots of travel, lots of rest and lots of changes.

Our annual retreat in Colorado Springs was interrupted by wildfires, but the PG Retreat Board quickly shifted us to Breckenridge, where we stayed in the clear Colorado mountains, realizing that while the setting matters, the most important part of the Retreat is coming together.

Following the Retreat, I journeyed to Ithaca, New York, for a lovely rest with my friend from high school and college who lives in a house in the woods. I loved waking up to bird songs and tall trees rustling in the wind; it was such a peaceful, restful stay, and a pleasure to be with someone who has known me so long.

I then spent a week at Chautauqua Institution by Lake Erie, living in a quaint, small New England village, where everything is walkable, including lodgings, food, all the classes, lectures, recitals, discussions and thought-provoking encounters that Chautauqua has been offering every summer for 100 years. It was a cross between a small town and a college campus, with everyone engaged in the space and the conversation. The theme the week I went was, "Inspire. Commit. Act." There were speakers who have done amazing things for our world. It was indeed inspiring. And I learned to play keyboard, which I have been wanting to do for years!

My last trip this summer was to Pinewoods Dance Camp in Plymouth, Massachusetts. As you all may recall, I went to Winter Dance Camp in North Carolina last year and found that I love to contra dance. This was a different setting: cabins in the woods, towering pines, luxuriant green moss, on a lake. I really love being in the woods! We danced in outdoor pavilions, which was lovely, but mighty steamy in August. Lots of grace had to be given to those gentlemen who had to change shirts three to four times each session! I met some wonderful people and plan to go to my next dance week, again at Christmas time, in Berea, Kentucky.

This year, for the first time, my children are in school. Public school. Adam is still taking community college classes (He *loves* his English professor, who offers lots of controversial topics and high-level discussions: perfect for Adam!), but the other three are in their zoned, local public school.

Jaron is in the IB program in ninth grade, which, after two weeks, he says is okay. I think he will be fine there once he makes friends. There is a large volume of work, which is brand new to him, but it is not difficult.

Derek and Evan are in the fifth grade gifted program. There could not be two more disparate responses. The other day when I picked them up, Derek said, "It was the best day so far!" Evan chimed in "It was the worst day so far!" This is typical of their personalities, so no surprises there. I am working with Evan to help him cultivate a positive outlook; Derek comes by it naturally, though he is certainly on a steep school procedure learning curve.

As anyone whose kids have entered school after homeschool has told me, the hardest part is navigating the classroom rules and procedures. As Derek says, "I can do the work, I just can't do it that fast!" Thankfully, they have an excellent teacher who has great control of his classroom, which makes a huge difference in their experience. There is no slacking, and there is no nonsense in the room. They love that environment. They will get the rest of it down too, eventually.

As for me? Well, between driving them back and forth to two different schools with two different schedules (Jaron does take the bus to school at 7 a.m., but I drive them the rest of the time. The bus was sensory overload for Evan and Derek, and just takes way too long to go three miles), I have a lot fewer free hours than I imagined I might. No complaints at all, happy to have the younger ones home until 9:15 in the mornings and Jaron in the car by 1:45 p.m., heading home. It gives me time to spend alone with Jaron in the afternoon…what a delight.

I hope everyone had a wonderful summer and is looking forward to my favorite season: crisp, clear fall. In Florida, fall is like spring up north: a chance to be outside again!

August 30

Medical Update

Well, I wish I could say I have news as good in this area as I did about my summer adventures…

After completing my chemo and radiation for lung cancer in February 2011, with a Cyberknife radiation treatment to the brain in November 2011, I had many months of good, clear scans, showing everything stable or shrinking. The scans I had a few weeks ago were not as kind.

There is active disease in my brain. Nothing like it was—just a few spots. I do have some swelling in my cerebellum, so have had to go back on steroids, and will meet with the Cyberknife doctor next week to develop a plan of action to address these few lesions and get the disease process back at bay.

Additionally, I found out that I have invasive ductal breast cancer, a small area in my left breast, which is very treatable with minor surgery. I have a consult with the breast surgeon next week to develop a plan for that as well.

Following those treatments, I will likely do another round of chemo for the lung cancer. Because I responded so well to treatment, because it has been a year and a half since I completed treatment, and because the cancer is active in my body, the doctors feel it would be the most prudent course of action to re-treat me and hope for a similarly remarkable response.

I share that hope, and ask all of you to join me in that belief. I would appreciate all your good thoughts, prayers and positive energy. Please feel free to share your sympathy and hope; please do not share any pity or distress.

As I have throughout the journey, I am looking to the positive. I am very grateful that the lump in my breast was not metastasized lung cancer, but a very treatable breast cancer. There will be a new set of challenges to face, but I am confident in my friends' and family's support and my own outlook to not only get through this, but to triumph!

December 13

Two Years!

Last week was the two-year anniversary of my lung cancer diagnosis. Every day is a great reason to celebrate; the milestones just remind us. I have been doing scans all along, and the last set, a few months ago, showed some possible activity in the chest, but it was hard to tell what was what because of all the scar tissue. So I opted to wait until the next scans and determine a course of action after seeing those. Well, that time has come. I had my scans two weeks ago, and the area they were concerned about has grown a bit and is more active than on the previous scan. So they're pretty confident that it is cancer coming back. I am going to start chemo again in January: the same protocol as last time, as that worked quite well at keeping the cancer at bay for these two years.

No one can really tell me how I will react to the chemo this time. The conventional wisdom is that it will be tougher the second time around. But I am not going to be on steroids, and I am not going to be doing radiation, so maybe it will be the same, or even better…we will just have to see how it goes.

The doctor did say that it was fine to wait until January so that I may have this month to enjoy the holidays and go on my scheduled trip to contra dance camp in Kentucky between Christmas and New Year's. It is a very odd sensation to plan to be incapacitated, or at best, tired. The first time around, it was quite a whirlwind; now it is more calculated.

The lumpectomy at the end of October went fine. The surgeon got clear margins from the lesion, and I am not doing any further treatment for the breast cancer.

Ironically, I am again the Event Director for our beloved PG Retreat, as I was when I first went through treatment. I had an awesome assistant then, and I am fortunate enough to have another awesome assistant this year. People ask me how and why I am taking this on. The truth is that it helps tremendously to have something outside of treatment to focus on, to pour my energies into, to think about. I have confidence that people will help me however they can, and will forgive me however I can't.

Over Thanksgiving, Adam and I were in San Francisco while Todd took the other kids up to New York. We visited Stanford and Berkeley; he loved the former, did not care for the latter. He was fortunate to have a friend from PGR host him for the night at Stanford. Though there were not many students on campus due to Thanksgiving Break, they did play a Monopoly game and go to a party. He loved riding bikes to breakfast and the professors he was able to meet. Adam is planning to spend the spring semester researching schools, and to go away to college in the fall of 2014.

I enjoyed spending one-on-one time with him. The first

time I was able to do that with any of the kids was when Jaron was nine years old; he and I went to Little Rock, Arkansas. That was a very special trip for the two of us. At one point, while we were visiting the Hot Springs, he suggested we sit down on some rocks and rest. Once I was comfortably seated, he said, "Mom, this is why I wanted us to take a vacation together. Because sometimes, you just need to take a break and sit, and I wanted to make sure that you had a chance to do that." While there, we mined diamonds in the only diamond mine in the U.S. from which you can keep whatever you find, visited the Clinton Presidential Center, watched a marathon from our hotel window, visited the State Capitol and shared milkshakes each night in a cute little restaurant we discovered nearby.

Two years ago, Derek and I went to Ft. Lauderdale for a Pokémon tournament, just the two of us. (Todd took Jaron and Evan to a concurrent tournament in Orlando, for they did not want to travel that far.) The car broke down halfway to Ft. Lauderdale, and Derek and I did not arrive until well after midnight. Derek was a real trooper throughout the ordeal, and despite this setback, said he was very excited to be on his first trip alone with me. As soon as we checked into the room, Derek pointed out that it would be the first night he had ever spent away from Evan in his life. He was excited at the opportunity.

Last summer, Jaron and Derek went to Camp Yunasa in Michigan for a week at the end of July. Adam was away at a bridge tournament. This was Evan's chance to have one-on-one time with me. I think he had always been more comfortable being home than traveling, as he could turn to his electronic comforts. He participated in a robotics camp 45 minutes away, and we enjoyed the car rides together. This camp was his first experience doing something on his own, being his own person. He did well, but was happy when Derek and Jaron came home.

Derek has asked me to take him (and maybe the other kids) to Maine or Nova Scotia this summer to see his beloved puffins. What a wonderful trip to plan and look forward to!

(Update from February 2013.) After much investigation, we have booked a trip to Newfoundland for a week at the end of July for Derek, Evan, Jaron and me. I am really looking forward to traveling with the three of them again. I hope to build on an experience from when we went to San Diego for the World Pokémon tournament in 2009. We were at the San Diego Zoo, having a wonderful time together. At lunch, Jaron said, "We really like you like this!" "Like what?" I asked. "Fun mom!" So I shall be fun mom again while we explore Newfoundland and see hundreds of thousands of seabirds, most especially the puffins.

Having a goal, or multiple goals, is a great technique to keep looking forward and not get stuck in the past, or even stagnate in the present (I know…stay in the moment…I will. But I can plan!)

January 6, 2013

Accept Your Circumstances—Then Tweak Them

It was two years ago when I wrote a post entitled "Redeem the Day." I had thought that would be an appropriate title for this post as well; let's see if another title presents itself as I write.

As I mentioned in my last post, I spent the end of 2012 dancing in Kentucky. I was first introduced to the contra dance community in December of 2011, and have continued to seek out various dance weeks to see which ones are best suited for me. While the dancing was fun, it took a few days at camp before I started to really enjoy myself. I was so discouraged after I had gotten lost on the way to classes a second time (the first time was at night in the sleet) that I called the airlines to ask what the change fee would be if I left early. It was a minimum of $150— absurd for a free ticket. I called my friend whom I planned to visit after the dance week was over, to see if I could go early to stay with her. I could not, as she already had other company.

Once I realized that changing my plans was not an option, I decided to change my attitude instead. Rather than "sticking it out" with classes I wasn't thrilled about, I switched and found ones I enjoyed more. I had wanted to try many different kinds of dance, but found that I really enjoyed contra best, so I stuck primarily with that. I had been annoyed at having to walk back and forth to my room between sessions; instead, I brought along my book in the bag I carried so that I could read for thirty minutes of downtime rather than idly wandering between buildings. And most importantly, I sought out the company I lacked. I really enjoy talking with people, and I was discouraged by the lack of socializing, save at meals. So I made it a point to talk to people more during sessions, and walk between buildings with someone.

When I spoke to Jaron that day, I told him of my experience. He laughed and said, "Of course, once you realize you can't get out, you find a way to make the best of it." He said he does this at Yunasa (camp) each year…it's a matter of psyching yourself. Evan did the same thing once he realized that he had to stay in school and that homeschool was not an option at this time. This is not to say that feeling trapped is a good thing (I feel strongly that it is very important to know there is a way out of an uncomfortable situation or else one feels helpless), but that accepting that you cannot change the situation (assuming it is not an intolerable situation) helps you change your attitude, find a solution, and hopefully even enjoy your circumstances.

I am grateful that I was not able to just bail out. I wound up having a wonderful time, including a delightful New Year's Eve, that I would have missed out on had I just given up. I am thankful to those who noticed I was down and encouraged me; it made a tremendous difference to have my mood noticed and addressed and know that it mattered. Further, it mattered a great deal to be acknowledged in the first place. It makes people feel special when they are noticed and acknowledged and told that you are glad they are there.

Rather than just coming and going throughout your day, tell people you are glad to see them. It can change their whole attitude to know they matter. Help someone feel special; what a gift you can give!

I am starting four rounds of chemo in a few days. I have kind friends driving me for this first round as I make sure that the treatment will leave me well enough to drive myself the subsequent rounds. Please keep sending all those positive thoughts!

Happy 2013 everyone! May it be a wonderful year for us all!

February 6

One More Step in the Road

I am pleased that I am halfway through this round of chemo (I've completed two out of four times). This is such a different experience than it was the first time around. I am only doing chemo, not radiation, so do not have to go every day, just three days every three weeks. I am able to drive myself, so am looking at the treatments as one more errand to do that day. Chemo is listed no differently on my calendar than "PGR Conference Call" or "Cirque Zuma" (an African variation of Cirque du Soleil that I am attending with Jaron next week).

Though I do have to schedule my calendar carefully to avoid going out the week after chemo due to lower blood counts and weakened immunity, I am not feeling very disrupted by the treatments. I still help Derek and Evan with their homework every afternoon (after they change out of their school clothes), still try to make dinner some nights, still watch movies and order pizza every weekend with the kids, and still happily schedule time out with my friends. Oddly enough, it all feels very normal.

As all things have their time, it was time for me to have treatment again. I don't feel angry or upset that the cancer popped up again. I knew it would at some point. I am grateful to have had a two-year respite, and to be able to treat it again. As my brother says, I play whack-a-mole.

While I have lost much of my hair, there is still enough that on most days, I don't wear anything else on my head. Some days I wear a scarf, and am happy to pull a few hair strands out from the edges.

Just as my hair began to fall out, I was introduced by a mutual friend to an author who had just published *But I Just Grew Out My Bangs*! She is a lovely woman and we connected instantly. As I read her book, I found more and more that we have in common. As I enjoy connecting other people, I am grateful when others connect me.

I look forward to our Second Annual PGR Women's Weekend in St. Petersburg, Florida in two weeks. Twenty of us will gather for laughter, conversation and a well-deserved break for us all. We get to be ourselves, without any attachments, for a whole wonderful weekend. May all have an opportunity to be unencumbered every now and then!

February 23

Right Place, Right Time

I am sure I have mentioned before my strong belief that the Universe puts people in our path at the right time. Though we may not recognize the reason initially, it eventually becomes clear, or sometimes it may not, but it is still for a reason.

This past weekend, I had the great fortune to spend the weekend in St. Petersburg with the PGR Women's Retreat. In addition to in-depth sharing of all topics, from kids and books to sex and dating, we toured the Titanic exhibit at a museum and enjoyed some delicious meals with engaging company.

Though I have seen the Titanic exhibit twice before, there were new quotes and stories I either had not seen or had not focused on previously. One difference was that a member of our group, who had organized the trip, had lost her great-aunt and cousins on the Titanic. To see the list of names that included her lost relatives was very emotional for her. It reminded me of when we had gone to Ellis Island and seen some of the names from my grandfather's family, except his story turned out well. I also saw the quote from Ida Strauss, whose persona I was given last time we toured the Titanic exhibit. She was the wife of Macy's founder Isidor Strauss. When she was given a spot in a lifeboat but her husband would have had to stay behind, she refused the spot and said, "We have lived together for many years. Where you go, I go." And they perished together.

I had known and been touched by that story before, but one I had not known, or was just not as aware of, was a first class woman passenger who had two boys, ages sixteen and fourteen. Because they were considered men and not children, they were not offered spots on a lifeboat. Rather than leave her children, the mother went down with her sons, holding one in each hand until they could no longer hold on, and drifted down into the icy water. I guess because Adam and Jaron are seventeen and fourteen, that story just got to me. The tale of the Titanic is a haunting one for everyone, but our group noticed that the story is of particular fascination to our gifted children. I am not sure why, but several of us shared how our kids had known every detail, including passengers, specifications of the ship and a chronicle of the disaster. Whenever I hear about an obsession with the Titanic (or the Hindenburg, though there is much less detail available about that disaster), I consider it an indicator to look further into that child's gifts.

My dear friend of twenty years, Lynn, joined us on the Retreat. I was very appreciative of her watching out for me, making sure I always had water, or a place to sit when needed. She went home with a tremendous amount of information and support, and a long list of what to research further. And serendipitously, our friend Kelly (also of twenty years) walked into the hotel lobby as we were having one of our many chats. Kelly was there for the weekend with her boyfriend, and insisted on making good her offer of a month earlier to set me up with her Reiki master for a session during the weekend. She had offered both the Reiki and a massage, but we are holding off on the massage until I am done with treatments, as it increases the blood flow and may interfere with the rate at which the chemo is supposed to work. When I said it was fine if we were not able to schedule the Reiki session until later, Kelly answered, "What are the chances for me to run in to you and Lynn in a hotel lobby over an hour away from home? Surely there is a reason." And I thanked her profusely for the reminder that we must listen to whatever the Universe has in store for us; there is a reason people are put in our paths at particular times and particular places. I thanked her for setting up the Reiki session for me and agreed that it would indeed need to be that weekend. I had chemo this past week, and was feeling very sore and achy, which I had not been after the other sessions, so was very grateful to have some healing energy directed into me.

On a different note, I was prompted by a friend to copy all of my videos onto DVD because the videos degrade after ten years or so. I had already copied much of our collection onto DVD several years ago, but had stopped recording when the tapes were in 2007, so still had a number of years to copy. These past few days, I have reveled in watching the kids in 2007. Not only are they incredibly cute, they are learning at an incredible rate.

Maybe I only taped the parts that were particularly good, but I think that what I have is a true sampling of how our lives flowed. If anyone ever questions whether or not homeschooling works, they need only watch these movies. There are games throughout: games that they play the traditional way, games for which they create their own rules, games they create and play together. Adam and Jaron were constantly teaching Evan and Derek: Jaron taught them drawing and painting, Adam taught them multiplication, they taught each other about space and geography. The level of interest and astonishment upon learning something new was incredible. Derek's face lights up as he reads the distance that the planets are from their respective moons, and from each other, "Is that a nonillion?" Evan successfully navigates a Lego car through a road and bridge created in a class with neighborhood kids several years older. Jaron crochets a yarn string that stretches across the whole house, up the stairs and around the corner. Adam plays Scrabble with Derek, helping him learn how to spell by giving him the word and the letters, but jumbling them so that Derek figures out how to spell the word.

I kept thinking I should go do something productive rather than watching these movies, but what could possibly be more productive than reliving such happy childhoods? Over the years, I vigilantly recorded our days, about an hour each month, and am comforted by this visual record of our lives.

I am currently an Application Reviewer for PG Retreat. As I watched those movies, I was reminded of situations and sure signs of their incredible development. I now know what it is I am looking for in the anecdotes the applying families share: that joy of discovery and learning from such a young age. I have a friend who is exploring the option of homeschooling her son, and who would appreciate support and "proof" to help convince her husband. Again, I am grateful to have been prompted to watch the movies—at the right time.

Added this afternoon at 5:00 p.m.

I just returned from picking up Derek and Evan from school. I was contacted by Evan's teacher this morning to please come for a brief conference this afternoon to discuss moving him *up* into the next reading group! (What a wonderful conference topic that would be!)

I go through the carpool pick up line 99 percent of the time, but today I parked so that I could meet with Evan's teacher. I had a piece of paper on which to take notes, and as I was leaving my car, the wind blew it out of my hand. As I reached down to grab it, or step on it to stop it from blowing away, a woman from the car next to me started to help me catch the paper. After we were successful in picking up the paper, I thanked her, and she said, "Is that you, Kapper?" There is only one person in the world who calls me Kapper, and that is my dear Angelina, who was in my peer counseling class when I last worked, as a guidance counselor at Gulf High, in

1996. It was Angelina, whose son is in the fourth grade gifted class behind Derek and Evan at school. They both know him, and have even done projects with him. We never once saw each other or knew the other one was there this whole year. It was only because I parked for a conference and the wind caught my paper that we saw each other now, for the first time in at least ten years. (We did keep in touch with holiday cards after she graduated.) She told me that she remembers when Adam had hiccups in my belly and the thrill she had when she felt that. She is now a pediatric nurse. I told her about the entry I had posted not twenty minutes before seeing her, about being in the right place at the right time. How cool is that?!

March 20

Integrity: Making Conscious Choices

Everyone knows that it is very easy to get caught up in the heat of the moment and do something one may later regret. Fewer people may realize that they have the option to make a conscious, preemptive decision that eliminates the possibility of what may turn out to be a wrong choice.

This conversation came up the other day with Jaron, when we were discussing some kids in his school who take drugs. He said he wasn't going to do that and had decided his stance in advance so that he would know his answer. I asked if they had been taught that through a drug prevention program, and he said no, he just figured it out for himself. I was so impressed that he had; I had done the same thing when I was his age.

This ties back to your self-perception. If you think of yourself as "a person who does not do drugs," then that is who you are. If you think of yourself as someone who goes along, or who is willing to try anything, then that is who you are. I am not judging it one way or another, just saying that if you want to think of yourself as a certain type of person, then you need to consider options and make choices in advance.

It occurred to me today that this same principle applies to a multitude of choices. I have not been feeling 100 percent these past two weeks, and do not feel that I should be driving at the moment. Derek and Evan were unhappy to take the bus back and forth this week. I got upset that they were asking me to drive them when I had made a conscious choice to not drive, and I felt guilty that I was unable to drive them. What I realized is that if I had not made a firm decision not to get behind the wheel, I likely would have given in and driven them, especially if I was feeling okay when the time came to leave for school. The thing is, it might have been five minutes later when my feet started to tingle or be numb, and then I would have had to drive home impaired. I told them that I would not jeopardize anyone's safety by driving when I was less than 100 percent. In order to ensure that truth, I had to make a pre-decided choice and stick to it, regardless of circumstance.

This smaller truth pervades many parts of our lives. If you do not want to yell at your children, you decide that you will not raise your voice, except in an emergency. If you want to be a valued employee, you will consistently make positive contributions, regardless of whether or not you are appreciated. If you want to be a kind and generous person, you will look for opportunities to be so, and not judge other people. Across the board, you will live as the person you choose to be and not allow temporary circumstances to affect the inner core of who you are and how you act in the world. It is a matter of integrity—consistently being the same person throughout all the parts of your life.

I recently read *The Man Who Quit Money*, and was struck by the conscious, conscientious choices that Daniel Suelo made when he chose to opt out of the money system. He could not keep a few dollars around for emergencies; he had to jump in with both feet. He had to find a way not to use any cash, nor earn any, yet still live a healthful, optimistic life. He did not give in to the temptation to accept any offering unless it was freely given with no expectation of exchange. Suelo was able to succeed because he made a decision to live in a certain manner, and did not deviate from that path. He remained true to his choices and found great peace in being congruent in all areas.

Life is much simpler when we are able to make some global choices in advance. This can be as simple as brushing your teeth every morning or as complex as treating each person you encounter with kindness and compassion, regardless of the situation.

March 24

Choose Which Events You See As a Stream

In the past two weeks, the following happened to different friends of mine: had a SWAT team situation in her home; visit to the emergency room for kidney stones; scammed by a longtime confidant; broke an engagement; stroke; daughter diagnosed with cancer; spouse took a severe pay cut.

During the same time, the following happened to different friends of mine: dramatic healing from a severe infection; decided to homeschool (right for *her* family); decided to have children attend school (right for *her* family); daughter accepted into the college of her choice; son accepted at top-notch theater arts school; son offered a ballet internship in Germany.

Personally, during the same time, I have had more side effects than after any of the other rounds of chemo. One quite serious, and several less serious side effects, different issues each day: muscle pain, headaches, joint pain, chills, sweats, and a racing heartbeat. My serious side effect was a probable TIA (mini-stroke). I had numbness and couldn't find many words, but thankfully an immediate brain MRI showed no damage, and I was better within an hour. I am on steroids and aspirin for now. And I am done with my chemo treatments.

During these same two weeks, Derek lit up like a kid in a candy store at the opportunity to watch history videos, Adam called me from a bridge tournament in St. Louis to ask for my advice on how to deal with some difficulty with a client, Jaron discovered quantum physics and ordered his own books from Amazon to understand the concept better, Evan chose virtual brain surgery and CSI simulations over Minecraft (at least some of the time), and I deepened my relationship with a wonderful man I have been seeing for a few months.

It is not a glass-half-full, glass-half-empty situation— it is more like when you buy a blue car and suddenly you notice all the blue cars on the road. You focus your attention on different events, running together a string of positive events rather than negative ones. Or vice versa. But really, how much better your life overall will be if you choose to see those positive events as a string rather than the negative ones.

March 28

Lots Of Options For a Family

When we first started acknowledging the trouble in our marriage, Todd and I read. A lot. We read books about how to improve/save your marriage and books about personal growth and satisfaction. He read some of my books about spirituality, and no longer dismissed them as nonsense. Finally, once we were done, we read books about divorce and children of divorce.

Ironically, one of the books I read was about a woman who was diagnosed with cancer, which prompted her to examine her life. She realized she was unhappy in her marriage and chose to leave after her diagnosis so that she could live her own life for however long she had left. Everyone told her she was crazy. She traveled and settled in a beach house, living her days simply and joyfully in nature. She was treated and recovered and met the love of her life at that beach. She chose to end her joyless marriage in favor of a chance at happiness. I thought to myself, "If that happened to me, I would choose to do exactly the same thing."

Todd was convinced that the kids would be damaged and would always be first and foremost Children of Divorce. I had spoken to many friends who had divorced whose kids were fine, often much better than fine. Words like resilient, persistent, and creative came up often. I read a particularly encouraging book that talked about maintaining family celebrations and events as a large extended family, with both parents and any other significant others. It sounded like more people to love.

We thought it would be least disruptive for the kids to remain in the house while Todd and I alternated living in it with them. We had read about this arrangement and it sounded plausible.

The reality has been nothing we could have ever read about. It may be unconventional (isn't my life?), but it works for us.

We all live together in the house: he lives upstairs in the master bedroom, where the kids' bedrooms are, and I live downstairs in the wing with Adam. We keep a common calendar so that we are aware if one of us has plans. The other one then has to work around those plans in their own schedule. We do errands for one another and maintain the household. But we each have a significant other (he for two years, I for two months), and maintain our own separate lives.

When the kids went to school this year, he was terrific about helping them with their homework as soon as he got home from work. In the beginning, they needed a lot of help, and he and I would each take a child to work with. While I mostly help them now (if they need it), he works with them on projects and occasionally, math. He puts them to bed each night after they come to my room and say good night to me.

I am thankful to have the situation we do. It is best for the kids to have two parents in the house. It is best for us to have a built-in backup. And the kids see that there are lots of alternatives that can work. I am not suggesting that this is something to aspire to, but if strange situations arise, strange solutions are called for. We are respectful of each other, and probably kinder to one another than we were before. We both always have the best interests of the kids in mind, which informs everything we do and makes choices easier. And the kids are indeed creative, resilient, and open to all kinds of families. I believe we have found a way to make it work.

April 1

Endless Possibilities

Just as our living situation has shown my kids that there are many ways to be a family, I believe that the years of homeschooling helped show them that there are many ways to be educated.

There is a movement afoot which decries college, at least in its traditional form. While I still believe in the idea of college, I do appreciate that there are more and more ways to get that degree.

A homeschooling friend's 16-year-old daughter spent this past year as an exchange student in Switzerland. This sounded like an amazing opportunity, so Jaron and I read the book she recommended which prompted her travels: *The New Global Student*, by Maya Frost. Jaron was so excited about the idea that he read the book each night before bed. He said he would love to do a trip like that.

The more I thought about it, the more I realized it was probably best to do it as a gap year rather than during high school. The main reason is that it would be tremendously hard to return to regular high school after having had an adventure in Europe for a year. Normal life would be intolerably boring in comparison. The other reason, in our situation, is that I need Jaron. Selfishly or not, I count on him for so many things that I am not willing to give him up until I have to. I rarely play the

Something Extraordinary

cancer card, but in this situation, I feel it is warranted. I cannot imagine choosing to lessen the time that I have with him. There are memories to be made, and I want to hold on to every day I can. Jaron agreed with my assessment of waiting for a gap year experience, and will consider that option rather than heading straight to college.

When Evan was struggling in school last fall, he would come home miserable every day and beg to be homeschooled again. When I answered that this was not an option, right now, it was much better than saying that it was not an option, ever. There is a sense of being able to get through anything if you know you have options. He was so unhappy for those first few months until we changed his placement that I was worried he might slip into depression. When he felt trapped in his situation, it was awful. But because we had homeschooled all along, he soon realized that there was an alternative. He knew that he was not really trapped; even if he had to wait a bit to improve the situation, there was a way out.

This realization that there are endless possibilities is, I believe, inherent in homeschoolers. That is why I feel we will always be homeschoolers at heart.

The kids were on spring break this past week. The very first morning, we sat at the breakfast table for over an hour, lingering after a leisurely breakfast, discussing quantum physics, the Roman Empire, and how light works. They quizzed each other with root words, world capitals, and complex math problems. It was as if they had built up all these intellectual inquiries and were so excited to have the time together to let it burst forth. Throughout the week, we watched history and science videos, played a four-day History of the World game that Derek created, along with many other games that we never have time to play. It filled my heart to know that even though they are going along fine with school, they have an insatiable curiosity that has not been squelched by school.

And Adam? He is one of the most unorthodox kids you will ever meet. I am incredibly proud of who he has become. His education has been cobbled together through both traditional and unconventional means. He took all his high school science through online virtual school and completed that by age thirteen. Then he took math classes at the local community college and finished Calculus II by the time he was fifteen. He is still taking community college classes; he has done additional science, and this year, English and psychology. He is taking Latin I and II online to complete his language requirement for college.

He continues to travel for bridge, both nationally and internationally. The other day, he said "I have some time in between tournaments this summer. I'm thinking about going to Europe for a few weeks and just exploring." He has been earning money playing professionally, so that part is taken care of. He would be fine just taking off on his own, although he would like a companion. It would be a great opportunity for him to travel through Europe before he goes to college the fall after next. The fact that he knows that this is a possibility thrills me.

Take a look at what you have always wanted to do, or explore something you never knew you wanted to, and realize that there really are endless possibilities.

April 4

Ethical Will

As this journal draws to a close, my journey is still in its infancy. What began three years ago as a gnawing sense that there was more to life than what I was currently experiencing, has proven to be more transformational then I could have ever imagined.

Throughout this experience, I have been grateful for my friends, grateful for my family, grateful for my medical team, grateful for each day.

While Adam, and later Jaron, have read much of this journal, Derek and Evan have not. They know that I am writing this book, and have asked if they too could read it. I explained that while they certainly could, there are some entries that they may not fully understand at this point in their young lives. I likened it to the suggestion that no one under 40 study Kabbalah (Jewish mysticism) because it is difficult to attain the life wisdom necessary to understand it before middle age. However, I did read through the entry regarding Derek's flow-of-consciousness conversation with him. We reminisced about that evening two years ago when we had that discussion. He remembered it, along with many other hour-long conversations we'd had in the evenings, a chance to reconnect after spending much of the day apart as I went through treatment.

After a particularly rough week, I recently wrote on Facebook:

> *Life is so good. When you haven't been feeling 100% and then all kinds of good things are happening, there is this synergy, and instead of life just being good, it is amazing. I am so fortunate to be part of such a wonderful community of people of integrity and character who just Do the Right Thing.*

I have written this journal to share my insights with everyone, but also as an ethical will for my children. An ethical will reflects the "voice of the heart." While I certainly hope and plan to be here to impart these thoughts personally, this book affords me the opportunity to put down in writing what I wish to leave as a legacy for them.

As Randy Pausch wrote in *The Last Lecture*, all of his insights were ultimately directed to his children, who were too young to fully understand and appreciate what he had learned through his journey, what he wanted to share with them for their life's journey, and what he may not be able to say to them as they grew up, possibly without him there.

To you, my children, I bequeath all of life's joys and blessings. May you always know how very much your mother loves you, forever and ever and always.

Loni Kaplan

Appendix : Resources

1. Giftedness

I have referred to my beloved PGR, which is Profoundly Gifted Retreat. If you have a profoundly gifted child, and are focused on developing the whole child rather than focusing on achievements (although those are welcomed too), please explore pgretreat.com, and if you think it is the right fit, come and join this amazing community.

To find out if your child is profoundly gifted, there is no better testing center in the United States than the Gifted Development Center in Denver, Colorado. I highly recommend it: gifteddevelopment.com.

If your child is gifted at any level, the best resource for all things gifted is hoagiesgifted.org.

2. Homeschooling

There are a tremendous number of resources for homeschooling and unschooling, both in books and online. While there are probably hundreds of books I could recommend, the three that stand out as having really changed how I look at education are *The Teenage Liberation Handbook* by Grace Llewelyn (first published in 1998; still a classic), *And the Skylark Sings With Me* by David Albert and *Homeschooling Our Children, Unschooling Ourselves* by Alison McKee.

3. Cancer

There are many cancer support communities online, which I found much more productive than attending a local support group, which was often filled with negative energy and pity. Particularly helpful were LungLoveLink and Team Inspire, which connect cancer survivors to one another for support and questions.

4. Divorce

The best book I read about divorce and children, the one that encouraged me more than any other, was *The Good Divorce* by Constance Ahrons.

If you would like to contact me with any questions or comments, you may email me at adamfolk@hotmail.com and I will happily respond.

Something Extraordinary